Grace
the *heart*
of the *fire*

Grace
the *heart* of the *fire*

milton jones

COLLEGE PRESS PUBLISHING COMPANY
Joplin, Missouri

Copyright © 1991
College Press Publishing Co.

Printed and Bound in the
United States of America
All Rights Reserved

Library of Congress Catalog Card Number: 90-86283
International Standard Book Number: 0-89900-393-1

dedication

*To Don DeWelt
who taught me how to pray
and gave me a heart for unity.
Grace has led him home.*

contents

9   foreword

11   Chapter One
are you saved?

19   Chapter Two
so simple a child could understand it

29   Chapter Three
does God grade on a curve?

39   Chapter Four
america's team

49   Chapter Five
don't fence me in

59   Chapter Six
out of bounds

67   Chapter Seven
grace or evangelism – can we have both?

77   Chapter Eight
blessing or oppressing?

89   Chapter Nine
bowling pins and archery targets

99   Chapter Ten
hitting the bullseye with our doctrine

109   Chapter Eleven
hitting the bullseye in our lifestyle

121   Chapter Twelve
hitting the bullseye with our message

131   Chapter Thirteen
swings vs. fire issues

foreword

Mystifying topic: grace.

The pragmatist fears it – it won't bring results.
The legalist loathes it – it fuzzies the lines.
The antagonist scorns it – it forgives too quickly.

Yet the sincere searcher thirsts for it, for grace is his only hope.

Grace. The incredible decision of God to save because of his goodness and not ours. The divine exchange of our problems for his perfection. The cross-granted, love-motivated, never-ending promise that God is on our side and in our corner.

Why do we fear grace? Why are we so quick to dilute the strength of God's promise? If we emphasize grace will we serve less? How can grace be used to motivate loyalty and not license infidelity?

These are some of the questions Milton Jones tackles in *Grace: The Heart of the Fire*.

Milton has masterfully taken grace from the status of the Sunday School and placed it in the Christian lifestyle. You'll find the book vivid, (concise chapters and clear illustrations), scriptural, (careful exposition of texts) and practical (specific questions which motivate).

If grace has been more mystifying than motivating in your life, then spend some time with this book – it may set your heart on fire.

Max Lucado

Chapter One
are you saved?

It was the most penetrating question I had ever been asked. It went right to the soul. I'm not sure how I had avoided it for so long. Maybe it had come in other forms on other occasions but never so stinging as that day.

I was a new student at Texas Tech University. Since I was a Christian and had not yet made many acquaintances, it seemed like a good idea to go visit one of the campus ministries. The haunting question was to emanate from the building that housed this campus ministry. They called it a "Bible Chair." In times past in Texas these buildings housed classes in Bible and religion that could be taken for college credit. Thus they had taken the name chairs of Bible. But in this case the credit class days were over, and campus Christians used the Bible Chair as a hang out for fellowship and fun.

When I first walked into the Bible Chair, a smiling coed greeted me and acted thrilled that I would have chosen to pay this place a visit. Patti asked the usual questions about hometown, major, dorm, etc. Then she dropped the bomb.

"Milt," she said. "Are you saved?"

She didn't ask if I went to church. She didn't ask if I was religious or even a good guy. Somehow she wanted to know the ultimate. She wanted to know if I had a glimpse of my eternal destination.

Why hadn't anyone asked me this before? I don't know. My church attendance had been impeccable. I knew by rote all the scriptures on how to become a Christian. I had become a Christian. I was a Christian. Why then was this such a difficult question for me?

I paused, pondered, and stumbled around in answering the question. Patti knew she had asked a good one. She could have let me off and changed the subject, but she didn't. Oh, I longed for one more question about my major. But the topic at hand was my salvation. "Was Milton Jones saved?"

I wanted to say "Yes!" but I didn't think that was true or an appropriate answer. I couldn't say "No" because that was to admit more than I was ready to reveal. And after all, I was a Christian. Finally, I was able to mutter a feeble reply. "I hope so" was the best answer I could conjure up for the most significant question of my life.

Where was the confidence of my salvation? Why wasn't there an assurance of the redemption that was supposed to have taken place in my life? Why didn't I feel saved?

Was my experience an isolated event? I don't think so. Too many people who have grown up in the church have shared a similar lack of assurance in their personal salvation.

My wife experienced a situation not unlike mine in her college career. Barbie was on a ski trip to New Mexico when everyone in the car expressed how glad they were that they could say, "I'm saved." Everyone, that is, except her. She was deeply disturbed that other Christians were assured of their salvation, writers of the New Testament were confident in their relationship with Christ, but she wasn't. Again, why was it that a person who had gone to church all her life, been baptized into Christ, and tried hard to serve the Lord couldn't voice the words, "I'm saved"?

Why is it that the very people who would agree most that they have the right way of salvation feel so lost? If this is true, maybe another look at the way we are saved would be in order. If the end result is that people feel lost after being saved, that should be a clue that something is truly wrong. If a person is a Christian, why wouldn't they feel saved?

Most likely church members don't feel saved because they either don't think that they are good enough or right enough. They have a view of salvation based upon their personal morals, works, and ethics. When they measure themselves, they simply don't measure up. They feel that they are not good enough to be acceptable to God. Therefore, they can't be saved. They usually have this hope that one day they will be better and then will be saved. But presently, there is always one more thing left undone, or another failure added to the many others that keeps them from feeling saved.

If it's not being good enough that is creating doubt, then it's usually that the person is not right enough. In other words, salvation is seen as correctness. The Christian always wonders if he has all of the truth and nothing but the truth in his doctrine. He fears that he may miss something. And if he is not right on everything, God will not accept him. From past experience, he has seen where he has been wrong before. He looks at other people and churches and finds their doctrinal errors. Could it be that he is the one along with possibly a few others that has finally discovered the truth? He hopes so, but there's still the anxiety that he may have missed a point. And would God actually save someone who is incorrect on something and not right enough?

Perhaps our lack of assurance stems from a faulty view of how we get right with God. It just might be that in our extended pursuit to find out how to be saved, we missed some of the essentials.

In my experiences in the churches of Christ, I have noticed something peculiar. As a group, we think we are saved. But as individuals, many feel lost. Saved as a group but lost as individuals – how can that be? Again it goes back to these faulty presuppositions about salvation. When we examine our group, we look good. As a group, it's hard to find anyone else who has higher morals and works harder. Surely God will save the group with the most commitment. As a group, it's hard to find anyone else who has gone to such an extreme to be right. Intellectually, it looks like we're closer to the truth than anyone else. When it comes to correctness, who could be more right? Comparatively, we excel in goodness and rightness – so our group must be the one that's saved.

Then why do we feel so lost personally? It's because salvation is a personal event not a corporate merger. Our salvation doesn't come from belonging to a group even if the group is the church. Our salvation comes through a personal redemption and a belonging to God. The church is not an organization to join to be saved. The church is the assembly of the people who are saved. If the individual members of the church do not believe that they are saved, it doesn't really matter what the corporate body says about itself. When salvation isn't personally owned, the church as a whole is in trouble.

We cannot earn our salvation. We may have figured that out with our minds, but many of us still have trouble capturing that with our hearts and actions. For too long, we have viewed salvation with pictures of a balance. We think that if we can get the good to outweigh the bad, then we will be

O.K. If I'm much more right than wrong in my beliefs, then maybe I'll be all right. But salvation is not found on the heavy side of the balance. If it were so, we would all share the burden of Belshazzar's indictment – "you have been weighed on the scales and found wanting" (Dan. 5:27).

When there is a lack of confidence in the salvation of Christians, evangelism also becomes very difficult. If evangelism is seen as a work of salvation to be good enough to God, then the motivation of leading the lost to Christ becomes distorted. Guilt motivates rather than gratitude. And it's difficult to convince someone of the way of salvation if you don't believe you are saved. Somehow, it shows through. The good news doesn't look that good.

Martha was raised in a Christian home in West Texas. She attended Bible classes and church services all of her life. When she was 12, she was baptized into the Lord. Upon graduation from high school, Martha went to a Christian college. From all appearances, Martha seemed to have the best spiritual influence available in the churches of Christ.

When Martha was 21, she received a special honor. She was chosen to be a hostess at an evangelistic exhibit in New York City hosted by the churches of Christ. With great excitement Martha went on a mission to a place she had never been before to share her faith. Martha had opportunities for outreach like she had never experienced in her life. She talked to an agnostic, a Buddhist, and people from all sorts of various religious backgrounds.

One day, a very expressive and happy lady came to talk to her. She proclaimed how wonderful it was to be saved. Martha agreed but did not have the same exuberance of her visitor. In fact, Martha was so unemotional that the lady thought something was wrong. Martha had learned never to trust her emotions in religion and figured that this lady was probably Pentecostal. The lady finally asked her: "Dear Martha, you do know Jesus has saved you, don't you?"

Martha replied: "I am a member of the Lord's church. Yes, I have obeyed the gospel. I have been baptized for the remission of my sins."

"I know, Martha, but I am asking you are you saved right now?" the lady asked.

Almost in tears, Martha responded: "I think so – I hope so. I try to be faithful to Christ."

The lady left disturbed that a young lady on an evangelistic mission could so deeply doubt her own salvation. How could she possibly be a witness for Jesus?

Martha was devastated by her experience. She wept, prayed, and hoped that she could have more faith. But a confidence in her salvation and a assurance of her hope in Heaven was something that she feared would never be available to her.[1]

How tragic! We can be confident in our salvation. The Apostle John wanted us to know that we are saved. "These things I have written to you who believe in the name of the Son of God in order that you may know that you have eternal life" (I John 5:13).

You can be saved. You can know that you are saved. Salvation doesn't come from being good enough or right enough. Salvation is a gift that comes by God's grace.

Questions for Discussion

1. Could you make the statement, "I'm saved!"? Why or why not?
2. What has kept you in times past from feeling saved?
3. How have you thought of salvation as being "good enough"?
4. How have you thought of salvation as being "right enough"?
5. What has been your motivation for evangelism?
6. How does a lack of assurance of salvation hurt our evangelistic efforts?

Endnote

1. Walter Burch, "Is Assurance Really Possible?" *Mission*, August, 1969.

Chapter Two
so simple a child could understand it

I can't remember what I used for sermon illustrations before I had children. Stories about my kids always seem so cute and interesting to me. There's no telling how many people I've bored with them. But the next time that I'm running dry for a story, my congregation will probably hear another one about Patrick or Jeremy.

Grace was my subject, and I needed a good illustration. Patrick was four but has always been a little bit advanced for his age. I was sure that Patrick couldn't comprehend grace but even a wrong answer would give me a funny story from the pulpit. As a result, I sought out my young theologian in pursuit of a definition of "grace."

"Patrick, can you tell what 'grace' is?" I inquired.

"Well, it's like this, Dad" he began. "You're an adult, and I'm a little kid."

I was tracking with him so far. "Yes," I said.

"Well adults have jobs and make money. Little kids don't."

I wasn't sure where this was leading, but I thought it was going to be interesting to find out.

"I want a Ghostbuster's Proton Pack. If you get me one, it will be grace."

Wow, did I ever walk into that one. It certainly would be grace if I got him that toy. But wait a minute, didn't he give me a pretty good definition? Patrick wanted something he could not obtain for himself. I had the ability to get it for him. He had done nothing to earn one. He hadn't even saved any money to buy one. He couldn't if he had wanted to. His only hope was getting the Proton Pack as a gift. And if I gave it to him, it was grace. He was right. It was another good preacher's kid illustration.

Getting the Ghostbuster's Proton Pack is a lot like our salvation. It was a good goal but it couldn't be achieved. We want to be saved but we don't have enough to pay the price. Our only hope is to receive our salvation as a gift. And that's exactly how the Bible says it happens.

Paul writes in his Ephesian letter: "For by grace you have been saved through faith; and that not of yourselves, it is the gift of God; not as a result of works, that no one should boast" (Ephesians 2:8-9). He tells us that grace saves us. It is not our works. Instead, salvation comes through a gift. Our salvation doesn't come as a result of anything that we have done or can do. Therefore, we have nothing to brag about when it comes to our part of the salvation process. We couldn't pay the price. God could, and He did with His Son. It was grace.

Grace is a gift – a gift that we don't deserve. It comes unexpectedly like a surprise. Grace is too good to be true, and yet it's true. When we were lost and couldn't do a thing for our salvation, God offered us the free gift of eternal life through His Son, Jesus.

Jack Paul, who was my campus minister at Texas Tech, was trying to illustrate this point to a class of college students. One young lady couldn't quite comprehend the message. Jack opened his wallet and pulled out the lone bill that was there. It was a twenty. He then turned to the girl and said, "Here's a gift for you, twenty dollars." She eyed the money, and then he asked her, "Did you do anything to earn this money?"

"No," she replied.

"That's right," he said. "You haven't done anything to earn it, but it's yours if you want it. It's a gift."

It was a good illustration of a gift that was not earned, but the little encounter went on to show the problem with grace.

Although Jack was freely offering the twenty dollars and would have given it to her, she just stared in disbelief. She knew there must be a catch. People do not give away money.

After a short while, Jack asked her, "Do you have the money?"

She responded, "No."

"Why not?" he asked. "You still do not have the money because you did not take it. You didn't receive my gift."

The young college student may not have been twenty dollars richer, but she did learn an important lesson. Grace must be received. It cannot be earned. It cannot be bought. But it must be received.

There's enough grace for everyone, but few have the gift of salvation. Why? They simply haven't received the gift of God's salvation. Because it seems unbelievable that God would give salvation, we look for another way or try to earn it for ourselves.

I once saw an acrostic for grace. It looked like this:

God's
Riches
At
Christ's
Expense

That's what salvation by grace is all about. We receive all of the marvelous riches of God's enormous bounty. And we don't pay for it, Jesus does. It doesn't seem fair. It's not. That's why it's grace. It doesn't seem believable. That's why it takes faith. Why would God do such a thing? That's easy – because He loves us. The explanation is found in

SO SIMPLE A CHILD COULD UNDERSTAND IT

the most popular verse in the Bible. "For God so loved the world, that He gave His only begotten Son, that whoever believes in Him should not perish, but have eternal life" (John 3:16).

With enough grace and love given for all, what a shame it is that not everyone will be saved. For one reason or another, people have not chosen to receive the gift, and the gift of salvation is only for those who receive it.

"But as many as received Him, to them He gave the right to become children of God, even to those who believe in His name" (John 1:12).

After being asked to speak on the subject of grace in Texas recently, I was told that people would enjoy my talks because grace was "in" in Texas churches. I wanted to say, "Well, it's about time!" but I was fearful that "in" might mean it's just the latest fad. Stanley Shipp, director of the Spiritual Internship in St Louis, once told me, in reference to some churches where he had been, that "Grace had often been a subject without ever being a lifestyle." I'm fearful that grace might be the topic that we talk about for the next few years before we move on to something else. For our survival and our salvation, my prayer is that grace will always be at the bedrock of our preaching.

In another day, grace wasn't "in" as it might be today. A preacher by the name of K.C. Moser championed the doctrine of God's grace every place he went whether it was received well or not. When I was in college, Brother Moser was still teaching and preaching. A group of us who were in college had the opportunity to literally sit at the feet of Brother Moser and learn from him every Wednesday night. Since I had just recently come to appreciate God's grace and this man had rooted his life in it, I wanted to glean any bit of knowledge that I could from him. I'll never forget his answer when I asked him to describe grace for me. He summarized his theology with the words of the song – "Nothing in my hand I bring, simply to thy cross I cling."

This understanding of God's grace is rare among any group of people. I recently heard an analyst of churches and religious trends state that he could find no one proclaiming a deeply rooted doctrine of grace. Instead, grace had been codified. He said that a movement needs to be started on grace because no one (all churches-period) is founding a movement on grace. In his analysis, instead of responding to God's grace, people are being bullied into the church. I think he's right. Wouldn't it be wonderful to see a great religious movement rooted in grace?

If we are saved by grace and not by works, it means that there is nothing that we can do to merit our salvation. Then where do our works fit into this plan? What is their purpose? After that great doctrinal statement of God's grace in Ephesians 2:8-9, Paul explains works in verse 10, "For we are His workmanship, created in Christ Jesus for good works, which God prepared beforehand, that we should walk in them" (Ephesians 2:10). It's clear from verses 8 and 9 that our works do nothing to save us. So where do they fit in? Paul states that "if any man is in Christ, he is a new creation" (II Corinthians 5:17). When a person is born again, he is a new creation. What is he created for? He is created for good works. His good works can't save him, but they are the very purpose for which he was recreated.

Because of God's grace, a Christian should be able to say, "I'm saved." In one sense, salvation can be seen as a past event. Most Christians would not be hesitant to say "I was saved." Salvation can be seen as what happened when you became a Christian and were baptized into Christ. We can look back into a point in time and know that we were saved then. In another sense, salvation can be seen as a future hope. We might say, "I will be saved." This statement admits that our salvation is not ultimately realized until we reach our heavenly destination. At that point, we will know that we will be saved forever. Examining salvation in the past or future is important but doesn't seem to be as threatening as looking at salvation as a present experience. There is a greater hesitancy to say "I am saved now." Part of the reluctance comes because it can sound like an arrogant statement. It is only an arrogant statement if you think you did something to deserve that salvation. When we understand God's grace, a statement of our assurance is not a boast of how good we are but of how good Jesus is.

In Romans 5:1-2 Paul describes salvation in the past, present, and future. "Therefore having been justified by faith, we have peace with God through our Lord Jesus Christ, through whom also we have obtained our introduction by faith into this grace in which we stand; and we exult in hope of the glory of God." He refers to his salvation as a past event when he speaks of having been "justified by faith." Salvation is seen in the future as he looks to the "hope of the glory of God." But Paul sees salvation as a present experience when he acknowledges "this grace in which we stand." We are able to proclaim salvation as a present experience for one reason – we stand in grace.

We say that we believe in God's grace, but I think many of us are still struggling with it. I said that it's so simple that a child could understand it. Yes, Patrick gave a pretty good definition. But it may be a lot like that tricycle I bought last Christmas. It was unassembled, but I didn't worry because the man at the toystore said that even a child could put it together. Maybe a child could, but this adult couldn't figure it out. The instructions didn't make sense to me, and I couldn't believe that it would go together like the blueprint pictured it. Maybe a child can believe in a simple gift of salvation that comes from God. But some of us adults have trouble with it. It's hard to believe and doesn't make much sense. When we look at our Bibles, it seems hard to comprehend that God could make it all fit together that way. But we must believe it. Again Paul says "For by grace you have been saved through faith."

Questions for Discussion

1. How would you describe God's grace?
2. Why can't we earn our salvation?
3. How do you receive God's grace?
4. Explain what grace as a subject but not a lifestyle would be like?
5. If we are not saved by our works, are they important? Explain.
6. Are you still struggling to believe in salvation by God's grace? Why is that?

Chapter Three
does God grade on a curve?

In his insightful little commentary on the book of Romans, *How to Be a Christian Without Being Religious*, Fritz Ridenour asks the question, "Does God grade on a curve?"[1] Do you remember what that means from your school days? Grading on the curve is where you compare your test score with the rest of the class. If you do better than the others, then you get the best grade. The worst grade goes to the one who does the worst in the class. You are not graded by what you actually made on the test but rather by how you did in comparison with everyone else.

Does God grade that way? Sometimes we act like it. It's as if God is looking down at us comparing each one of us with each other. If we do better than most, then we get into heaven.

When we operate like God is grading on a curve, we set up scales for performance by which we judge people. Some people set up a morality scale. People then are judged by how good or bad they are. Their works are evaluated, and if they are ranked high according to the general population, then surely they will get into heaven. Others set up fruit-bearing scales. I've seen this done in highly evangelistic ministries. Christians are evaluated by their performance in leading the lost to Christ. The more you win to the Lord, the higher you rank on the scale. Those that are the most evangelistic must be the ones who are saved. Then, there's the accuracy scale. You are right with God based upon your accuracy in understanding everything God says in the Bible. The one who figures out everything exactly like God intended it gets the highest grade. The saved become the people who have best figured out a religious, intellectual jigsaw puzzle. And if you miss very many at all, you will probably rank too low to get a passing grade and be saved.

There have been all kinds of religious curves that have been set up. It would be difficult to count all the scales that have been created for judgment. There is, however, one overwhelming problem with these scales – God doesn't grade on a curve.

Let me explain this in baseball terms. I am a Seattle Mariners' fan. I'm one of the very few long-term fans. Being a Mariners fan has been difficult because in their first 15 years of existence, they have never had a winning season. And yet I still went to the games.

Opening night for the Mariners is always my favorite game. It's my favorite because the Mariners are still in contention. I hate it when the Mariners open on the road. By the time they get back to Seattle, they are historically out of the race.

Well, it was opening night for the Mariners at the Kingdome. The season was beginning in Seattle. Attired with my baseball cap and shirt, I sat in the stands on the first base side of the field with grand illusions of Seattle winning the pennant this year. As I sat there, I began to root for one of the Mariners to get a hit on his first at bat. Because if he got a hit on his first at bat in the first game of the year, the lights would flash 1.000 for his batting average on the huge scoreboard when he came up for his second at bat. I had never seen anyone bat 1.000. The first couple of batters made outs. Then, Alvin Davis came up. He did it. He got a hit. He was batting 1.000. Anxiously I waited to view the words "DAVIS - 1.000" on the Kingdome Diamond Vision scoreboard. When his second bat came up, I couldn't believe it. There it was – "DAVIS - .999." The scoreboard only had 3 places for a batting average. In stark reality, it made me realize that no one bats 1.000.

No one in baseball bats 1.000 for very long. No one can get a hit everytime. Not even Babe Ruth,

Mickey Mantle, Lou Gehrig, or Reggie Jackson. No one bats 1.000. No one since Ted Williams has batted over .400. If you bat .358, you probably have a chance at being the batting champion in the major leagues. If you bat .258, you have a chance of being in the majors (especially Seattle). If you go down to .158, it's probably down to the minors for you. But no one bats 1.000.

What's your batting average in the church? Many of us tend to look around the body and judge people by their batting averages. She's having a good year. Her attendance is up, her contribution is up, and she even makes it to ladies Bible class. She's batting .301.

But if you think your acceptance with God is based on your batting average, you better bat 1.000. James says "For whoever keeps the whole law and yet stumbles in one point, he has become guilty of all" (James 2:10). James says that if you don't bat 1.000 by the law, you are lost. It really doesn't matter if you bat .358 or .158; if it is not 1.000, you are lost.

With God our goal is not batting 1.000, but it's righteousness. But just like batting 1.000, no one is righteous. It's stated plainly in Romans 3:10: "There is none righteous – no not one." What a discouraging statement! The goal is righteousness, and no one makes the goal. This is why we must depend on the grace of God. It is our only hope.

Are you batting 1.000 in the church? No. Are you righteous before God? No. What do you do then? Paul makes an interesting statement in reference to Abraham in Romans 4:3: "For what does the Scripture say? 'AND ABRAHAM BELIEVED GOD, AND IT WAS RECKONED TO HIM AS RIGHTEOUSNESS.' " Abraham wasn't righteous but he was counted as if he was righteous. He was "credited" as being righteous. This is a business term with which most of us are familiar. It would be like my writing a check for $10,000 when there was only 98¢ in my account. You know well what is going to happen to that check. It would be counted as insufficient. But what if as the check was going through the bank, the president tells the bank to go ahead and count the check as if it's good. He says that he will credit the extra $9,999.02 to my account. In other words, he credits my account for what is not there. I don't have the money, but he acts as if I do.

Righteousness is very similar. None of us are righteous, but God counts us as if we are. He credits us as righteous when we are totally insufficient. Romans 4:23,24 tells us the crediting was not just for Abraham. It was for us too. "Now not for his sake only was it written, that 'IT WAS RECKONED TO HIM,' but for our sake also, to whom it will be reckoned, as those who believe in Him who raised Jesus our Lord from the dead."

Why would God count us as righteous when we are not? Maybe the best explanation of this is found in Galatians 3:27 - "For all of you who were baptized into Christ have clothed yourselves with Christ." Here Paul helps us understand one of the most important aspects of our Christianity. When we are baptized into Christ, we are clothed in Him. Therefore, when we become Christians we are in Christ. We are not righteous but we are in the only one who walked the face of the earth who was righteous – Jesus. We are counted as righteous because we are in Him, and He was righteous. And the best part of being "in" Jesus and counted as righteous is found later in the book of Romans. "There is therefore now no condemnation for those who are in Christ Jesus" (Romans 8:1). When we are "in" Jesus, there is no condemnation. I can know that I am saved not because of my works or righteousness, but because of His. Therefore, again we see that to say that I am saved is not a boast at all of my own goodness or righteousness but a boast of that of my Lord.

Now if all of us fail to perform (bat 1.000) in our walk with God, what should that tell us? It should tell us two things. First of all, it should make us quit trusting in ourselves and what we are going to do for salvation. I'm not going to be saved based on how good I am. Are my works important? They certainly are. That's what my new birth created me for, but still not one of them counts for my salvation. I'm also not going to be saved based upon how right I am. Should I seek to be accurate in my doctrine? Absolutely! But just as I fail in my works, I will also never be perfect in my knowledge and correctness. If I have to be absolutely right on everything, I will be lost. I need God's grace not only because of my lack of performance but also for my lack of knowledge.

Secondly, my failure to bat 1.000 in my spiritual life should make me quit comparing myself with others whether outside or inside the body. This becomes a futile exercise if we're saved by grace. Yet, we still do it. We compare ourselves with others in the body and decide if we're doing better or worse spiritually than they are. In fact, many see their goal as being the batting champion of the church. They evaluate themselves as batting a spiritual .375 when the closest brother to them is only batting .310. They then think God must certainly be pleased with him for doing so well.

I've also seen churches try to compare themselves with other churches. They want to have the highest team batting average. They think that they are better than other churches because they score higher as a congregation on whatever scale it might be, whether souls won or sound doctrine.

Comparing with one another whether it be churches or individuals leads to an unhealthy competitiveness. It ultimately causes division.

One of the greatest reasons that these types of comparisons will not work is because we may not use the same criteria for figuring batting averages. In baseball, they have it down to a science. But in the church, we might not all agree on what it means to be fruitful. Differing opinions will, without a doubt, occur when we try to measure who is sound in their doctrine.

If God is so gracious to us, don't you think we could be more gracious to each other? Shouldn't that be the proper response to grace? It's time we start working together in the church. Maybe we need to be more like a team. But let's not do what some baseball teams do. As soon as someone hits a slump, "Get rid of him!" they cry. "Send him down to the minors!" That's what we've done with many of our preachers, isn't it?

Batting averages are going to fluctuate, even our spiritual ones. We need to change our tactics. When a brother or sister is low and not performing as in past days, we shouldn't kick them off the team, trade them, or run them down. The New Testament teaches us to encourage one another. Grace should produce graciousness. If we all have to bat 1.000, then none of us could play on the team. But if grace is the rule of the umpire, maybe even you and I can play. Need a right fielder?

Questions For Discussion

1. Have you ever acted like God graded on a curve? Explain your answer.
2. What have been some of the criteria used in setting up scales for judgment in your church experience?
3. In what areas have you personally tried to become perfect in order to gain God's acceptance? What happened?
4. To whom do you have a tendency to compare yourself in the church? How has this proven futile?

5. Explain what it means for you to be "in" Christ.
6. How could you be more gracious and encouraging to your brothers and sisters in the Lord?

Endnote

1. Ridenour, Fritz. *How to Be a Christian Without Being Religious.* Ventura: Regal Books, 1967.

Chapter Four
america's team

America's team. You know who it is, don't you? Everyone in Texas did on that day, or so they thought.

While speaking to a group of college students from Abilene, Texas, I mentioned that underneath my sweatshirt was a teeshirt with the logo of America's team. Everyone began to smile. Instantly, there was an incredible bonding as they all envisioned what must be on the front of my shirt. It had to be the lone star of the Dallas Cowboys.

During the Seventies, the Cowboys had become such a successful and popular football team that not even Dallas or Texas was believed to be a big enough designation for their loyal supporters. No, they were America's team.

As difficult as it was going to be, the time had come to reveal my shirt to all these onlookers. When I removed my sweatshirt, the students' faces were as puzzled as could be. Some said, "What?" Others said, "That's not America's team!" A few of them were irritated, and a couple downright mad. Most thought it was just a joke.

What was on my shirt? A huge picture of the face of an awesome looking bird. And underneath the logo, it said "Seattle Seahawks."

Quickly the students explained to me that the Seattle Seahawks were not America's team. Everyone knew that the Cowboys were America's team (at least in Texas).

After their protest, I explained to them that it wasn't a joke. Seattle really was America's team. In the past, the Cowboys had referred to themselves as America's team. Since everyone had not agreed with their designation, some criteria for evaluation was needed. It was decided that whatever NFL team sold the most merchandise with their logo on it must be America's team. This was a good criteria for Dallas because every year they sold more shirts, pennants, souvenirs and other paraphernalia than any other team in the NFL. At least they had until that year.

Yes, that was the year of a big surprise. There were more sports souvenirs sold bearing the Seahawk name than any other team. Because of the hype of Brian Bosworth's going to Seattle coupled with the losing season of the Cowboys, Seattle's name had outsold that of Dallas. The Cowboys could no longer meet the requirements to be America's team.

After my talk, I was enlightened by a diehard Cowboy fan. He simply said, "That's not how you measure America's team!" It didn't take me long to figure out how he would measure America's team — any way that made Dallas come out on top.

I grew up in Texas being a Cowboys fan. When I left Texas, it was hard for me to believe how unpopular the Cowboys were in other areas of the country. In fact, it was hard to find anyone neutral about them. People either regarded them as America's team or the team they would most like to see lose in the NFL.

My teeshirt experience taught me a lesson. Everyone wants to claim to be America's team. I also learned that people will quickly set the criteria for being America's team if you will let them.

It's not a large jump from comparing football teams to comparing churches. I'm beginning to think that everyone wants to be America's church. In other words, they want to be that number one, ever successful, and most popular church. If they are not seen that way, then they usually want to change the criteria for measurement. If they are a large church, then America's church should be measured by the attendance. If it's an evangelistic church, the measure will be by conversions. When the church is small, the measure becomes soundness or whatever other element in which they deem themselves to be doing well.

But isn't this all folly? We have learned that God doesn't grade on the curve with individuals. (He doesn't with churches either.) The church in Sardis thought it had everything going for it. But God said it was dead. It's measurement was not the same as the Lord's.

Anytime we start comparing ourselves with other people, we are going to get into trouble. Paul said "We do not dare to classify or compare ourselves with some who commend themselves. When they measure themselves by themselves and compare themselves with themselves, they are not wise" (II Corinthians 10:12). Paul's message is clear – when we get into this comparison game, we simply are unwise.

We have been playing the comparison game for a long time. It started with the old "my dad is bigger than your dad" argument. That conflict of childhood was just spiritualized into "My church is bigger than your church." Comparisons, generally, don't help us find the truth. Most comparisons that I've seen in the church usually cause hurt and division. It's true that sometimes one person is right and the other is wrong. But truth is best discovered by looking at the Word as an isolated source rather than making a comparison with someone else.

When Paul makes his statement about comparison being unwise in II Corinthians, he is in the middle of a heated conflict that is not too dissimilar to many today. Paul is under attack from some church leaders in Corinth who think that he is not successful. He refers to these leaders as "super apostles" (11:5).

These super leaders have painted Paul as an inept leader who cannot measure up to their standards of success. Paul's theme in chapters 10 – 13 is a call for an evaluation of what our main goal is – success or maturity. Needless to say, Paul opts for maturity (13:11). Although it is conceivable that Paul could beat them at their own game of boasting, he thinks that it is foolish (11:17). Again he states, "We do not dare to classify or compare ourselves with some who commend themselves. When they measure themselves by themselves, and compare themselves with themselves, they are not wise" (10:12). In other words, if a person compares himself by himself, he cannot see the total picture. His judgement will be skewed. Obviously, a person will pick criteria for comparison that slant the picture in his favor. If a person gets to choose weapons, won't he pick the one with which he's most likely to win?

Success has become too important to individuals and churches today. It's difficult to distinguish some sermons from positive motivational speeches for successful living that could be heard in a sales seminar. Success by the world's standard, is not the goal of the Christian. Jesus would have hardly met the world's picture of a V.I.P. This fascination and obsession with being a success has clouded the viewpoint of what is most important in our faith.

D.A. Carson commenting on the relevancy of the problem in Corinth in II Corinthians 10-13 to our situation today states:

> We increasingly inhabit a time and place in Western history when humility is perceived to be a sign of weakness; when meekness is taken for a vice, not a virtue; when puff is more important than substance; when leadership, even in the church, frequently has more to do with politics, pizzazz, and showmanship, or with structure and hierarchy, than with spiritual maturity and conformity to Jesus Christ; When the budget is thought to be a more important indicator of ecclesiastical success than prayerfulness; and when loose talk of spiritual experiences wins an instant following, even when that talk is mingled with a scarcely concealed haughtiness that has learned neither humility nor tears. To Christians hungry to understand and repent of these evils, 2 Corinthians 10-13 speaks with rare power and passion.[1]

The problem of the super apostles could best be called "spiritual one-upmanship." It was a religion rooted in success. They simply wanted to be one-up on Paul when it came to measuring their leadership. Why this becomes a bone of contention is because they don't measure each other by the same criteria.

Church leaders today are also guilty of measuring each other's leadership. Sometimes it's done by morality. Other times it's by fruitfulness. A comparison of academic degrees is frequently used on one another. Too often it's numbers, or if not that, it's soundness. Now, the standards in Corinth that were most important to the super apostles had to do with some Hellenistic standards of rhetoric and their visionary enthusiasm. That's how they measured success. Again it was a religion rooted in what their society said comprised success rather than one shaped by the gospel. And when these criteria of their culture were used, they thought that they were one-up on Paul.

Even today, we christianize culture. Whatever our culture says is successful, we try to imitate and spiritualize. As an example, in the eighties, many church leaders tried to christianize the yuppie. The intensive, driving, bigger is better philosophy that marked the yuppie was often used in the church as an example of success. Instead of business being the arena for success, some individuals have used religion as their vehicle to success. They applied their intensive driving spirit on the church and found a spiritual way to promote themselves.

What leadership characteristics would it take to impress a church today? Many churches haven't shown that much concern on whether their minister prays, reads his Bible, or treats his family well. That's not how they evaluate success. No, it's whether or not he can deliver a good sermon and make the church grow. What has impressed the religious world today is not character, integrity and humility. Instead it has been resumes and eloquence. True, it's the way of the world, but it's become the way of the church too.

The super apostles of Corinth were not that different from the health and wealth gospelizers of today. They quickly touted themes that put power, winning, triumph, and success in the forefront. However, they sorely negated or put on the back burner the characteristics of compassion, meekness, humility, patience and service.

Spiritual showmanship was simply not the mark of leadership or the way of the cross to Paul. According to Paul's outlook, one doesn't come to know God from a position of arrogance. Does that mean that Paul would not boast? No. However, Paul wanted to make sure that there were some ground rules laid down in the area of boasting.

Can you boast and not be a fool?

Paul thinks so. The problem is not with boasting but with the subject of one's boasting. According to Paul, there are two proper ways to boast. First of all, one could boast in his own weakness. "If I must boast, I will boast of the things that show my weakness" (II Corinthians 11:30). In today's world of self-realization and be-all-you-can-be promotion, these words are very odd. Paul boasts not of his triumphs, abilities, and position. No, he boasts about his weakness, sinfulness, and need. He might outdo the honors when they're for someone else (Romans 12:10), but not for himself. When it comes to his life, he practices what might be called a one-lowmanship.

The other area of Paul's boasting is in the Lord. "But, 'Let him who boasts, boast in the Lord' "(II Corinthians 10:17). His message is about how great God is rather than about promoting himself.

What do you boast about? We could all use a self-analysis to see what comes out of our lips. When we are talking about accomplishments, who do we boast about? Is it the Lord? If not, Paul would tell us that we are being quite foolish. And everyone should have known Seattle was America's team all along.

Questions for Discussion

1. How do churches compare themselves with each other?
2. What are the world's standards for success? How have these been displayed in the church?
3. What would a "super apostle" be like today?
4. What characteristics should mark a spiritual leader?
5. How have you practiced spiritual one-upmanship in your past?
6. What do you boast about? Are you different from the apostle Paul? Explain.

Endnotes

1. Carson, D.A. *From Triumphalism to Maturity*. Grand Rapids: Baker Book House, 1984.

Chapter Five
don't fence me in

The God that holds you over the pit of hell, much as one holds a spider, or some loathsome insect over the fire, abhors you, and is dreadfully provoked: his wrath towards you burns like fire; he looks upon you as worthy of nothing else, but to be cast into the fire; he is of purer eyes than to bear to have you in his sight; you are ten thousand times more abominable in his eyes, than the most hateful venomous serpent is in ours. You have offended him infinitely more than ever a stubborn rebel did his prince; and yet it is nothing but his hand that holds you from falling into the fire every moment. It is to be ascribed to nothing else, that you did not go to hell the last night; that you were suffered to awake again in this world, after you closed your eyes to sleep. And there is no other reason to be given, why you have not dropped into hell since you arose in the morning, but that God's hand has held you up.[1]

Does that excerpt from a sermon motivate you? If you believed it, you would certainly be motivated. Jonathan Edwards preached this famous sermon, "Sinners in the Hands of an Angry God," and started a great revival in the 1700's in colonial America.

Many of us grew up on hellfire and damnation preaching. And when it's time to get something going or get the people to moving, we might think that it's time for the preacher to pull one of those old time revival sermons out of his file again.

Probably all of us have been the recipients, or possibly the victims, of a damning sermon. Why have they been used so often? It's because guilt motivates us. Hasn't it worked on you before? Don't you remember that time when the preacher straightened you out by scaring you with the fire of hell if you did not change? And maybe you did change as a result. Judgment is real, and fear is a valid motivation.

However it is often unbalanced, unwarranted, and unappreciated. It's true that we need a greater understanding of God's wrath, but there are other motivators. And some motivations are greater than guilt.

Grace is a great motivation, but I think that we are afraid of grace. Why would we be afraid of something so good? Recently someone told me that if we emphasized grace too much, he was afraid that we would all become spiritual pansies.

It makes sense to fear something evil or scary. But why would you fear the lamb rather than the lion? Although it seems odd, I think it's true – grace scares us. Guilt bothers us and tears us up, but grace scares us because we don't think it's enough.

Paul seemed to think that grace was a great motivation. "But by the grace of God I am what I am, and his grace to me was not without effect. No, I worked harder than all of them—yet not I, but the grace of God that was with me" (I Cor. 5:10). From this passage, we can see how Paul had the proper response to grace. When he realized who he was, the least of the apostles, and yet was given the abundance of forgiveness and blessings, the impact was immense. The result of grace for Paul was not a small motivation; it produced the hardest worker.

If we rely on grace, many are afraid that we won't do much as a Christian. To get results, guilt will motivate more than grace (at least that's how we act). But according to Paul, grace should produce more work. A better understanding of God's grace should lead people to working harder in the church, being more evangelistic, reading their Bible more, and better church attendance. In fact, if these are not occurring there is probably a lack of an understanding of God's grace.

Another reason that people are fearful of grace is the belief that without a stricter code, a license to sin will be created. Grace becomes scary because it appears that there are not enough rules to keep people in line.

Again Paul dealt with this dilemma of grace. In Romans he states "The law was added so that the trespass might increase. But where sin increased, grace increased all the more, so that, just as sin reigned in death, so also grace might reign through righteousness to bring eternal life through Jesus Christ our Lord" (Romans 5:20-21). The problem, according to Paul, is that historically grace has increased proportionately to an even greater extent than our sin. If this is true, what is to change our behavior? If one truly understands how much grace God gives, wouldn't a person take advantage of it? Wouldn't he be slack in his lifestyle knowing that there is always easy forgiveness? This is why Paul poses the question of Romans 6:1; "What shall we say, then? Shall we go on sinning so that grace may increase?"

But to Paul, this is irrational thinking. It is totally contrary to a proper response to grace. He replies to the question, "God forbid." Or as the Phillips translation renders it, "What a ghastly thought!" To associate grace with a motivation to sin was an inconceivable thought to Paul. In fact, grace should produce the exact opposite response.

In his letter to Titus, Paul writes, "For the grace of God has appeared, bringing salvation to all men, instructing us to deny ungodliness and worldly desires and to live sensibly, righteously and godly in the present age" (2:11-12). Paul here explains that grace doesn't make one want to sin but encourages us to say "No" to our sin.

What Paul realizes is that a life in God's grace is on a much higher plane than one rooted in sin. When a person lives in grace, he has no desire to stoop back down into the worldly passions of the past. When a person tastes the riches of grace, he will be glad to leave behind his former ungodly desires. They simply cannot compare with the blessings of God's grace.

In Paul's eyes, grace leads to the hardest worker and the purest life.

Another reason that we are afraid of grace is that it doesn't spell everything out. In other words, there are not enough rules. It's true that we complain frequently about all of our religious rules, but most of us are comfortable with them. The removal of rules opens up a greater freedom, but it also is scary because the boundaries aren't as clear.

In Jesus' day, the Pharisees had a root problem that was similar to this fear of grace. The Pharisees loved God's word, and they wanted to protect it. A fear of God and a lack of understanding His grace compounded their problem. Because of this fear, they developed a system to meticulously obey the Scriptures. They were determined not to break a single law from His Word.

To make sure that they never disobeyed the Law, the Pharisees came up with a system to keep them from even coming close to angering God. They made a fence of Pharisaic rules for protection. These rules were like a fence around the Law.

If a man could keep the rules of the fence, it would guarantee a safe distance between him and breaking the laws of God. The fence became insurance. If you kept it, then you were assured that you didn't even get close to angering God by disobeying His rules.

The most obvious place where the Law was fenced was concerning the observance of the Sabbath Day. Since God had given instructions not to work on the Sabbath, all kinds of fences arose to make sure that nothing remotely connected to work was done. To pick some grain was like harvesting, which was work. Nails were not in sandals because that could be construed as carrying a burden. One wouldn't want to spit because the spittle could roll in the dirt which would be like plowing a furrow.

These laws were known as a *seyag*, which meant fence. The fence kept a person from getting close to the law. The problem was that these rules fenced some people out.

The difficulty of the fence was that people tended to focus on the fence more than the commandment of God. When arguments occurred, they were more often over the fence than what God had actually said.

When people focus on the fence rather than the true commandment, they never mature. They remain shallow because they don't focus on God's word but rather on man's. Maturity comes when disciples know how to think rather than just what to think. The Hebrew writer impresses this on us –

"But solid food is for the mature, who because of practice have their senses trained to discern good and evil" (5:14). Maturity comes when a Christian can look at God's word and then make a proper discernment in his situation on what's right and wrong. If a disciple never has to discern on his own but simply has all the decisions made for him by a fence, he will never mature. In fact, he never has to do any deep examinations into the character and nature of God. There is no need to – everything is spelled out in black and white.

I saw a good example of fence building in campus ministry a few years ago. A popular fence became the practice of double dating. Double dating would reduce the temptations of immorality in relationships with the opposite sex. However, the Bible doesn't teach double dating. Would it be acceptable? Yes, God gives us that freedom. Would it be wise? It probably would be in certain situations. But is it a commandment? No, it is not. When this fence of double dating became firmly entrenched in ministries, it became more of the focus of relationships than what God actually did say about purity. What became tragic is that some enforced breaking the fence with equal judgment to breaking the law. Often times students would get into trouble with their ministers or peers if they ever broke the fence even when they had not broken the law. In other words, they had gone out on a single date but had remained pure according to God's law. The result of fences is that they usually become more important than the actual law.

Footloose, the popular movie of a few years ago, dealt with a fence found in many fundamental churches. The fence was dancing. I can't remember a bigger deal made out of anything than dancing when I grew up. But dancing, whether you like it or not, is still a fence. The commandments are against lust and immorality. So should a teenager go to a dance? Maybe or maybe not. What he shouldn't do is break God's commandment.

I saw an unusual thing happening with the fence of dancing when I was a teen. We heard that there would never be a praying knee connected to a dancing foot. But in reality, some did go to dances and not give up their praying. We also heard that if you went to dances, you would lust and probably commit fornication. But in reality, some went to school dances and those sponsored by churches and did neither of these. Here's where the problem comes with a teenager or anyone young in the faith. He has been told that if you break the fence, you will break the commandment. But when he broke the fence, he discovered that he didn't necessarily break the commandment. Once he had broken the fence, he still had the free will to choose whether he would break the commandment or not.

This can be very dangerous. It is dangerous because sin has its consequences. When a person breaks a commandment of God, he will face consequences. However, he will not face the consequences when he breaks a fence. Here's where things get fouled up. If a person discovers that what he has been taught about the fence is wrong, he will probably disregard the fence. But he may also disregard the commandment related to the fence. When a person discovers that what he has been taught concerning the fence is wrong, he then doubts the integrity of the teacher. If what was said about the fence was wrong, then why should he believe what was said about the commandment?

I saw this very sequence of events happen frequently among young people in church. It happened with such issues as dancing. They would break the fence (dancing) and not sin. Then they would doubt the integrity of the church's teaching and break the commandments relating to purity. As a result, the teacher could now say dancing led to immorality. But is that what really happened? Dancing could lead to immorality but it doesn't always. What bothered me most was seeing young people leave a church because they doubted the integrity of its teachers. Their doubts started and were led too far by focusing on fences.

What needs to happen with young people is a focus on the commandments. They also need to learn how to discern between what is right and wrong. There are too many gray areas today to build enough fences to cover them all. If people really understand God's teaching on morality and want to do His will, they can learn discernment. If they find themselves at a dance, they will either leave because of lust or stay because they are not bothered by it.

Our present day fence-building is so very similar to that which Jesus deplores in the gospel of Mark, "Neglecting the commandment of God, you hold to the tradition of men" (7:8).

All of us are going to have traditions and ways of doing things.

Some will be good. Others will not be so good. For us to keep harmony, we must always go back to God's Word. If it is a tradition, does it in fact relate to the commandment? Or is it merely a fence? Most of our church divisions occur when we focus on a fence.

Please, don't fence me in.

Questions For Discussion

1. How do hellfire and damnation sermons affect you?
2. What is scary about freedom?
3. How should grace motivate us to be harder workers? Be specific.
4. Where has grace taught you to say "No" to temptations?
5. What are some modern day fences in religion?
6. How can discernment be developed without fence building?
7. Where have you gone too far in your life by throwing out the commandment with the fence?

Endnotes

1. Edwards, Jonathan. *Basic Writings*. New York: New American Library, 1966; p. 159.

Chapter Six
out of bounds

Sports Illustrated had captured another intriguing moment in sports. The scene was on the gridiron. It was the opening kickoff of a 49'ers game. Derrick Harmon had fielded the kick – but he was inches from the sideline.

The photograph heightened the suspense because not only were his toes up against the sideline, but his body was leaning over the out of bounds territory. In fact, in that stop action photograph, you could almost feel his body teetering over the line. Looking like one of those cars balancing on the edge of a cliff, the scene was perplexing. Would he stay in or would he fall out?

But the greatest aspect of this picture was the

people's eyes. The player with the ball had his eyes glued to his toes. The referee could look at nothing but the line. Even the tacklers were looking down to see where he stood in relationship to the line. All eyes were on the line. Did he fall out? I don't remember. I'm not even sure they told the reader. But for an instant in football history, nothing seemed more important than looking at the line.

After observing that photograph, I was reminded of Asaph in Psalm 73 when he stated "Surely God is good to Israel, to those who are pure in heart! But as for me, my feet came close to stumbling; my steps had almost slipped. For I was envious of the arrogant, as I saw the prosperity of the wicked" (v. 1-3). The psalmist pictures himself off balance when it comes to where he stands spiritually. It is as if he has his toes right up to the line that marks the division between the pure and the wicked. And he's not even sure himself on which side of the line he will fall. In our own lives, the law is like the line that our toes are pushing up against. We know where we are supposed to stand, but there is an enticement on the other side. Therefore, we keep our eyes glued to the line, inching our feet closer to it. We keep getting as close to the edge as we can without crossing over it.

There's a difference in fence building and line looking. Fences are built to keep us as far away as possible from the law. We fence the law because we are afraid people are going to break the law. Fences are bad because they are not the law and can create a focus other than what God has actually said. But the reason fencing is so popular is a valid one. We do break the law. The heart is deceptive and tries to run right to the edge of the line and frequently goes over it. The lure of sin intrigues us with the edge of the law.

Paul examines this dilemma in Romans 7 where he states:

> What shall we say then? Is the Law sin? May it never be! On the contrary, I would not have come to know sin except through the Law; for I would not have known about coveting if the Law had not said, "YOU SHALL NOT COVET." But sin, taking opportunity through the commandment, produced in me coveting of every kind; for apart from the Law sin is dead. And I was once alive apart from the Law; but when the commandment came, sin became alive, and I died; and this commandment, which was to result in life, proved to result in death for me; for sin, taking opportunity through the commandment, deceived me, and through it killed me. So then, the Law is holy, and the commandment is holy and righteous and good (v. 7-12).

We are like children with boundaries. As soon as parents lay down the boundaries, the kids go to the limit to check them out. The children could have been having fun playing in the house until you told them they couldn't go outside. Then they run up to the front door and stand there looking outside. We are that way with sin. We try to get as close to sin as we can without sinning. We want to run down the sideline trying not to step out of bounds when the middle of the field is open.

Our fascination with the line is most vividly seen in dating relationships. Teenagers ask the question, "How far can I go on a date?" Then we try to help them arrive at certain steps that are permissible until they get to the one step at which they must stop. The problem with this kind of advice is that it sets our children moving the wrong direction. We set them up on a step by step course where each move is closer to the line and progressively harder in which to say "No". The question should never be how close can I get to sin without sinning. Rather, our focus should be on how close can I get to God. This is the response of grace.

The problem of getting close to the line is that the area near the line is, as Asaph warns, very "slippery." Once we run toward the line, we are usually moving downhill. With each step we are trying to justify our own actions. But justification never comes with our own rationalistic stamp of approval. Justification is found in being on the field. God, the referee, decides who is in bounds.

The most talked about article ever published in *Leadership* was written by "Name Withheld."[1] We don't know the author because of the revealing intimacy of this leader's struggle with sexual sin. "The War Within: An Anatomy of Lust" tells the downfall of a well-known herald of the Bible into the dark world of pornography and other immoral activities. Although the writer knew it was wrong and tried to say "No," he kept crossing over into the impure. What helped to bring him out of his obsession with sexual sin was very interesting. His change didn't come with another "No," but with a resounding "Yes." The turning point began with a focus on Jesus' words in the beatitudes: "Blessed are the pure in heart, for they will see God." These words gave him the striking revelation that his sexual sin was keeping him from seeing God. It was as if there was vast and immense knowledge and intimacy available with God that had been totally hidden from him because of his sin. It was when he pursued God from deep in his heart that he was able to pull out of his immorality. The desire for God crucified the control of sin. Again it is a response to God's grace and character that shapes our morals more than any self-denial or imposed rule.

I've studied and written much on the subject of discipleship. In my examination and evaluation of it, I have seen discipling relationships frequently abused. It usually happens when one person starts trying to control the life of another. Often, he will put down rules that are fences rather than law. On other occasions, he will become an enforcer that never allows the other to respond personally from his own heart. If there is any one verse that has been used for a pattern of discipleship, it is II Timothy 2:2: "And the things which you have heard from me in the presence of many witnesses, these entrust to faithful men, who will be able to teach others also." In fact, this verse has been called the multiplying verse. It shows how faith is multiplied through four spiritual generations from Paul to Timothy to reliable men to others. The good thing about discipleship as a method is that it works. The bad thing about it is that it works no matter what the content. It works not only with Christianity but also with harmful cults and even multiple level marketing groups. For this reason, Paul doesn't begin his example of discipleship with II Timothy 2:2, but with II Timothy 2:1: "You therefore, my son, be strong in the grace that is in Christ Jesus." Discipleship without a strong foundation in God's grace can multiply error and legalism. The only thing more dangerous than being weak in grace is being weak in grace and multiplying.

Our greatest danger is not in crossing over the line – because at times we are all going to sin. Our greatest danger is to run away from God's grace. The problem with running to the sideline is that we turn our backs on God. When we live a life where we are merely trying our best not to step out of bounds, we are doomed to failure. When we head back toward the field of God's grace, our focus is no longer on the edge of failure. With eyes focused on God, we not only find forgiveness but also motivation to stay away from the line.

Missing God's grace caused the most severe dangers in the Book of Acts. The harshest rebukes of God came to the people who missed God's grace – Ananias and Sapphira in Acts 5 and Simon the Sorcerer in Acts 8. Ananias and Sapphira's rebuke of death came when they said that they had given something that they had not given. Simon's chastisement from the apostles came when he tried to acquire through his own means what only God could give.

These are the two most dangerous things that we could ever do. First of all, we could be like Ananias and Sapphira and say we have given something to God that we have not given. In their case, it was money that they said was given when in actuality, it was not. But it doesn't have to be money that causes this danger. It could be any work that we assume to have come from us when it has not. Most dangerous would be to presume that we have given some act of righteousness that makes us acceptable to God when indeed we neither have not nor could not.

The second mistake is that of Simon when he tried to purchase the power of the Holy Spirit. He assumed that he could acquire a gift of God by his own resources. We do this all the time – even with our salvation. But no gift can be purchased, and even making the effort to do so is condemned.

It's dangerous to fall out of bounds. But it's even more dangerous when you don't have anyone to pick you up once you have fallen out.

Questions For Discussion

1. What things entice you to want to cross the line into sin?

2. Have you ever tried to get as close as you could to breaking the law without breaking it? Give an example.
3. When you get close to the edge, do you usually stay in or fall over the edge? Why is that?
4. Are most discipling relationships that you have observed rooted strongly in grace? Explain your answer.
5. What do we often say that we have given to God when in actuality we have not?
6. What do we often presume that we can obtain from God by our own resources?
7. Why is it most dangerous to be weak in grace?

Endnote

1. Name Withheld. "The War Within: An Anatomy of Lust," *Leadership*. Fall Quarter, 1982, pp. 30-48.

Chapter Seven
grace or evangelism - can we have both?

There's something that I've noticed about churches that really bugs me. Evangelistic churches tend to become legalistic, and churches that allow a lot of freedom tend to lack commitment. Maybe this is a generalization, but it's been common enough in my experience to at least think about it. Although it's a situation that I don't like, I think I'm beginning to understand it.

When we are evangelistic and proclaiming to the lost that there is a way of salvation, it forces us to draw some lines. We have to figure out who's on God's side and who's not. Somehow you have to decide who is a Christian and who is in the right state in reference to the Lord's judgment. Otherwise, we are at a loss in how or to whom we communicate the gospel.

But where do we draw those lines? If we are not careful, we will draw those lines very tightly and only include ourselves. It's easy to do that. We want to include only people who are just like us or extremely close because then it is obvious who is in and who is out.

But can't this produce a narrow exclusivism? And couldn't this exclusivism backfire on our evangelistic efforts in the long run? I've certainly seen this in my church heritage, the Restoration movement.

The situation has happened too often to me. We are out on some kind of an evangelistic effort. Upon talking to someone about the Lord, he asks, "What church are you from?"

And after telling him, too many times I've heard the response – "Oh, aren't you the ones that believe you're the only ones going to heaven?"

Now, has that reputation really helped or has it hindered evangelism? Our attempts at sharing the good news haven't been seen as very good to many people. I'm afraid that too often we have shown a judgmental, sectarian spirit in our outreach that ultimately has turned people away rather than bringing them to the Lord.

Incidentally, have you ever thought about this? What if the Lord turned out to be more gracious than you thought He was? Would that bother you? I'm afraid that some people would be mad if others got into heaven that they didn't think were going to make it. Doesn't that reveal something about our hearts? If this upsets us, it shows that we are more concerned with being right than we are in desiring people to be saved.

When we become evangelistic, there is a tendency to enforce gray areas and impose rules that aren't necessarily in the Bible. Why is that? I think it's because a growing, evangelistic church becomes so full of new people who simply don't know how to live and act as Christians. But does that justify a legal system?

Our problem is that it takes a lot of time and effort to bring and equip people to maturity. And if you have new Christians running out your ears, how can you devote enough of yourself to training these people in how to discern God's will? What it boils down to is that it is much easier to tell people what to do than to teach them how to think. It also takes a lot less time.

When there are many new Christians around, often there is the fear that this group could get out of hand very easily. Therefore, we need to keep them under control. How are you going to do that? Set up as many rules that cover as many areas of life as you can. Then enforce them. In that way, you can remain in control of the situation. The only problem is that God was supposed to be in control – not us.

To teach someone how to think and help them learn how to discern God's will requires a lot of patience. It will never happen overnight. Freedom must be allowed, and that means there's going to be some mistakes made. There's also the possibility that if I teach and allow someone to think, he might not always agree with me. If we don't agree on everything, then how can we function together? Freedom poses some challenging and often times scary perplexities. That's why we keep enforcing our rules. It keeps things under control – our control.

The enforcement of man-made rules to maintain order is not our only problem. We also like to put a lot of stipulations on other people because of one of our greatest sins. We like to dominate people. We've been doing this all of our lives. Working hard to get our own way has been a lifelong habit for most of us. Through years of practice, many of us have become masters of manipulation. We manipulate by exerting force or withholding favor. Others do it in a quiet, passive and subtle way. They nicely talk us into submission to their will. We have become experienced at this. We started it with our parents. We threw tantrums, withheld affection, were overly cooperative — whatever it took to get our own way. That dominant spirit has been with us for a long time, and it is very easy to use it to get our agenda with people in the church.

When we manipulate and dominate people, we have made ourselves lords. Our ministry is not to get people to do what we want them to do or obey our rules. It's to help them to do what God wants them to do and obey His rules. Jesus is Lord, not us. I'm tired of church leaders lording over the flock. Peter said it wasn't to be so (I Peter 5:3).

GRACE OR EVANGELISM – CAN WE HAVE BOTH?

There are too many church leaders today who enforce their own rules, traditions, and desires as if they were God's. When you don't buy into it, you either can't function in the church or are treated as a second class Christian. It shouldn't be that way. The leader who tries to dominate others and denies another's spiritual freedom is the problem. He is letting his basic sin of having his own way rule the church. This not only ruins the leader's soul but causes great immaturity in the body. When his spirit is duplicated (as it always will be), the church becomes full of chaos, strife and division. We've seen it happen far too often. We need a greater freedom in Christ than many of us have ever seen. We are never going to agree on everything, but that's not what our unity is based upon. God's spirit keeps us one even in the midst of diversity.

But getting freedom will not always be the answer. Because on the other side of this whole issue is an equally disturbing problem. Why do people with great amounts of freedom tend to abuse it? Why is it that people who have experienced great doses of God's grace do so little with it? Have you noticed this too? Shouldn't a message of unmerited salvation and a law of love provoke an unyielding commitment?

I remember an intriguing statement that Tony Ash made in a National Campus Ministers' Seminar. He said, "I'd like to go to a liberal church of Christ where everyone came back on Sunday night." Tony was humorously expressing the same frustration. Why can't the ones who have discovered more freedom also show more commitment? Why is it that the ones who probably haven't as deeply discovered God's grace act so much more committed?

You would think that after hearing about the freedom that we have in Christ and His marvelous grace that great works would come simply as a grateful response. With such a great message of good news, it would seem certain that everyone would be out spreading the word. Missing an assembly would seem unheard-of to one who finds freedom. Wouldn't he be so filled with joy that he would have the deepest desire to be with others who have experienced the same salvation? It should be that way, but normally it isn't.

Freedom in Christ has often been interpreted as freedom to do whatever we want to do. When it doesn't appear that a resident policeman is on our case to keep us in line, we have taken great liberties to run beyond where some limits certainly must be. We recreate the situation that Paul discusses in Romans 6:1 – "What shall we say then? Are we to continue in sin that grace might increase?"

Why do we take grace as a license for sin? Why wouldn't we have the obvious response to grace and forgiveness? Why do churches that preach against legalism not grow more? Maybe in our response to freedom, we have become too independent. Freedom in Christ should produce some independence from law and sin, but it also should create a greater dependence upon the Lord. I've often wondered if independent churches don't produce independent people. A non-denominational, autonomous congregation is very healthy. But it may attract and create independent people. It's true that we want to be free from man-made religious systems, but we certainly don't want to have an independent spirit. Our freedom in Christ should produce a greater dependence on Him and His family.

When a person has been burdened with legalism and finds freedom, he usually decides that he needs to start making some choices for himself. He can no longer let the traditions or the leaders of the past control him. He has to take responsibility for his decisions. That sounds good, but one must be very careful that when he rejects legalism, he doesn't rebel against all authority. The goal of freedom is not to get away from all commandments. Rejecting legalism should move us toward a greater submission to God's authority – not toward a rebellion from any structure. Perhaps one of the greatest appeals of freedom for some people has not been spiritually based. Its appeal has been more as an avenue of escape from commitment or burnout. Freedom became the message rather than freedom in Christ. As a result, great works weren't the result because there wasn't a motivation coming from a deep gratitude. Inactivity became the result because one finally found a way out of the burdens of the system. But the way out was really more of an escape than a finding of God's grace.

What am I looking for? I'm wanting to see a grace-centered evangelism. Shouldn't those who have found God's grace be more evangelistic than those who are burdened down with legalism? I think so. I'm looking for a freedom in Christ where there is commitment. I want to be a part of a group of people who want to share Jesus simply because they want to share Jesus. I want to be a part of a body of people who want to have a high moral character because they personally have decided to be like Jesus. I want to be a member of a church where people make their own decisions, and they decide to attend all of the assemblies.

What I'm talking about has been referred to as balance. Maybe it's what Jesus called a narrow way. It's probably not to be found on the left or the right side of things. A razor's edge in the middle might best locate the way. Few have found it. I hope I do.

I hope you do.

Questions for Discussion

1. How have you seen evangelistic churches become legalistic?

2. Where have you observed a lack of commitment in some churches that have found freedom?
3. How have we drawn lines too tightly? Where have we not drawn them tightly enough?
4. What are some ways to keep from having a judgmental, exclusivistic spirit when we are sharing the good news?
5. When teaching new Christians, how do we get them to think rather than merely enforcing our rules to keep them in line?
6. If you have discovered God's grace, what needs to change in your personal commitment?

Chapter Eight
blessing or oppressing?

It was a phone call that I'll never forget. I received it from a young lady. She called to ask me what time she should fly from the East coast into Seattle. I couldn't figure out why she wanted my opinion. She said that her discipler had told her that she should be submissive to church leaders in Seattle while she was there. As a result, she wanted to know when she should book her flight. I told her that I didn't care and trusted her to make a good decision. She said "trust" wasn't a word that she heard much anymore.

Why would someone let another person control their lives? How could one turn over even the mundane choices of life to another person? I can understand why people might want to control others. It comes from a desire for power and a lack of dealing with one's own pride. But what makes people think that it is acceptable for someone else to set rules for her life? It's especially interesting to try to comprehend how this could happen in a Christian context.

I think that this whole problem can better be understood if we examine how differently Christians may view commandments. It is possible that someone who grows up in a Christian environment will see commandments very differently from a new person in the church.

Many of us who grew up in church never had a very good knowledge of God's grace. Justification may have been seen merely as keeping a lot of rules. I remember well my first public prayer. It had a sentence in it that still haunts me – "Dear Lord, help us to all earn our way to Heaven." Was I taught that? Perhaps not, but it was still my perception of God's way of salvation. When it came to entering the pearly gates, I had to have gone through all the right steps, done the right things, and if my works were good enough, God would accept me. It was a revealing prayer, but hardly the request I should have made from the Almighty.

But what happens to a person who has never quite comprehended the grace of God and then discovers it suddenly? This is what happened to me when I went to college. A campus ministry at Texas Tech exposed me to the marvelous riches of God's grace. Salvation was taught to me in a totally different light. It was not by my merit but by the merit of Christ that I was saved. It was too good to be true. At first, I couldn't believe it. But I checked it out. It was true.

In our campus ministry, it was so thrilling to see students who had gone to church all their lives first discover the grace of God. We found that when you finally discover God's grace, however, it's easy to swing so far the other direction that you only talk about grace and end up disregarding commandments. For some of us salvation becomes more feeling oriented than fact oriented. In our great desire to secure a greater confidence in our salvation, we went to the point of giving some people what had to be a false assurance.

What is the purpose of a commandment? Until we comprehend the aim of a "Thou shalt," we will never be able to put together an adequate theology of God's grace. God gives us commandments to bless us. We usually don't look at it that way, but it's true. God's commandments are not to weigh us down but to bless our lives. God's commandments are blessings. God gives us commandments because He loves us and wants what is best for us. He knows that if we obey His commandments, we will have the greatest joy.

God doesn't tell us not to commit adultery to spoil our fun. He knows that we will be happier in the long run if we are faithful to our husbands and wives. God sees all the wrecked marriages of the world and knows what has caused them. He tells us to be pure because he knows that we will have happier marriages, and our lives will be spared the grief of broken relationships and divorce. God realizes the guilt that accompanies cheating on a spouse. Therefore, He gives us the commandment because He knows that if we keep it, we will be blessed.

God doesn't say don't murder just to give us another rule that we have to obey. It's obvious the blessings that come when people obey this commandment. Our society is protected. We don't have to fear walking down the streets. Think of all the grief and anxiety in our land today simply because some are not obeying this commandment. Obedience brings blessings, and the more we obey, the more we are blessed.

God doesn't say to go and make disciples to burden us down with a difficult job. Again, it's to bless us. Fulfilling the Great Commission gives us a purpose in our lives. God knows that we will experience a joy like no other when we see others give their lives to Christ. I've heard people say – "Don't tell me that I have to be evangelistic. That's legalism." I think they have missed the point. Evangelism and the obedience to the commandment come from gratitude and an expected blessing. The person who says that he doesn't have to be evangelistic to be acceptable to God is really the legalist. He has simply lowered the standards for his legalism.

Evangelism never merits our acceptance before God, it is only the proper response of a grateful disciple.

BLESSING OR OPPRESSING?

God doesn't tell us not to forsake the assemblies because He loves hearing the statement, "I have to go to church." He tells us to meet with our brothers and sisters in the Lord to bless us. He knows that we need fellowship. God understands that we are much better and stronger together than apart. It's a blessing.

God can see the end. Because we can't, we often trade a temporary pleasure for the unending joy.

If you were asked to name the worst, most sinful city in the Bible, what would you say? Sodom would be my first choice. Sodom was that terribly wicked city that Abraham pleaded with God to save. After bargaining from fifty down to ten, God agreed to save Sodom for the sake of ten righteous people. But they could not be found, and Sodom was destroyed.

If you were asked to name the holy city of the Bible, what would come to your mind? It's Jerusalem, of course. But Jeremiah 5:1 has clouded my view of the great, holy city. "Roam to and fro through the streets of Jerusalem, and look now and take note. And seek in her open squares, if you can find a man, if there is one who does justice, who seeks truth, then I will pardon her." God gives Jeremiah the bargaining conditions for the salvation of the holy city, and it's not fifty or even ten righteous people. It's one. Jerusalem, the home of the priests and prophets, was so bad not one righteous person could be found. Now look at verses 30 and 31. "An appalling and horrible thing has happened in the land: The prophets prophesy falsely, and the priests rule on their own authority; and My people love it so! But what will you do at the end of it?" What a question! "What will you do at the end of it?" God can see the end of it. That's why He gives us all of His commandments. Since He sees the end, He tries to keep us from ruin and despair. He tells us the way to avoid destruction. He directs us through His commandments. When we follow them, we are blessed.

Much of our reaction to God's commandments is directly related to our view of the church. And it might not be simply our view as much as our first viewpoint. When you first saw the church and were exposed to God's commandments – was it a blessing or oppressing? Did the statements of God seem like they were going to bless your life? Or did they appear to be an oppressing factor that was keeping you in line?

Many people who grew up in the church knew the commandments of God all of their lives, but they didn't appreciate them. Commandments came across like rules to curb one's lifestyle. Because they had never experienced much of life outside of God's family, they wondered if there wasn't something out in the world that they were missing. It seemed that there was an alluring attractiveness out there that Christians could never experience. Again we see this as the Psalmist expresses in Psalm 73:2-3, "But as for me, my feet came close to stumbling; my steps had almost slipped. For I was envious of the arrogant, as I saw the prosperity of the wicked." Today people are like the psalmist. They think that there is something out there that they want to do but can't because they are Christians or from a Christian home. Therefore, the church and commandments may have been seen as oppressing to them before they were ever seen as a blessing.

Later in the psalm, we see how God's commandment to avoid the world was always a blessing. "When I pondered to understand this, it was troublesome in my sight, Until I came into the sanctuary of God; then I perceived their end "(Psalm 73:16-17). It is only through God's vantage point as the psalmist sees in the sanctuary that one can see the end. Whether a matter is a blessing or oppressing can ultimately only be determined by seeing the end of it.

As a campus minister, I saw hundreds of children who had grown up going to church leave their homes and go to the university. Many of them left the Lord quickly, and I witnessed very few of them returning. Most of them went the way of the world. They wanted to taste the temptation that previously had been restricted from them by their upbringing. They saw the church and the commandments of God not as a blessing but as oppressing.

The experience of someone not raised in the church may be drastically different. When you come from the depths of Satan's camp and follow the standards of the world for a long time, commandments may look different to you. If you have seen the falseness of the world and have been close to seeing the end of it, a commandment to live your life differently may not be oppressing. When someone who has realized their lostness finally finds truth as seen in God's commandments and evidenced in the church, he will probably regard his discovery as a blessing.

God's commandments are a blessing to someone who has no hope. When you know that your path and the way of the world goes nowhere, you welcome a new structure to your life.

A group of college students at the University of Washington asked me to talk to them about dating. They were all new Christians and had never been on a date that would have been remotely pleasing to God. They had decided not to date until they could know how to approach a relationship with the opposite sex with purity. After expressing Gods commandments on relationships, purity, and sexuality, they were overwhelmed with excitement. They thanked me. Now they were ready to date. It was a blessing.

A few months later I was asked to speak to some students at a Christian college – also on the subject of dating. Nearly all of these students had grown up in church. I made the mistake of using my same notes and making the same points that I had to the other group. This group thought I was a prude. This was the same stuff that had been handed down to them all of their lives. Wasn't there something new? They thought inside of themselves that there might be another way that was more fun and would make them happier. The commandments were oppressing.

The group that had seen the end thought the commandments were a blessing. Those that wondered if the world didn't have a better way merely saw them as oppressing.

God's commandments are needed for us to know how to live. When we don't obey them, we don't please Him. I'm not saying that if we obey them all that we merit our salvation because we can't obey them all. We haven't even come close. But we still obey to please God, and we obey because we believe it will turn out best for us.

Do you see the commandments of God as a blessing or do you see them as oppressing? If you grew up in a church and didn't get heavily involved in the world, what a blessing! That's the way it's supposed to be. Don't feel intimidated because you don't have a dramatic testimony about how you left all of the pleasures of the world. Just be thankful for a Christian heritage that spared you a lot of grief. If you are from the world and finally God's way and His church was revealed to you, what a blessing! You've found a treasure. Keep following God's commandments, and you will be blessed.

Now if a commandment becomes a blessing, it's easy to take another commandment from someone (not out of the Bible) and suppose you will be further blessed. People who are new in their faith are very susceptible to this. They have found that God's commandments bless them. They have received these commandments from older Christians. If these older Christians add some commandments of their own, the new Christians will probably obey them simply because the other commandments which were given turned out to be a blessing.

The problem is that God's commandments will bless you, but mine will ultimately burden you down. Because of their lack of biblical knowledge, new Christians will have difficulty distinguishing between a biblical and an extra-biblical command. Too often in evangelistic ministries leaders will tell the message as more than is really there. They add to it to keep control. The new Christians readily and happily receive all the commandments because they assume that they will be blessed by their obedience. Maybe they are at first, but in the long run, the commandments of men start burdening them down. The great danger is that a person frustrated and burned out may disregard all of the commandments instead of merely rejecting man's.

Today's society has molded people into undisciplined and unstructured lifestyles. When an alternative is offered which provides a meaningful structure to life, people are often willing to buy into a lot more than what God prescribes. Our task is to discipline ourselves as a church and not require what God has not required. That may take some immediate changes.

Questions for Discussion

1. Did you first see the church as oppressing or as a blessing?
2. Where did you first discover the grace of God?
3. What are some ways that we have traded an unending joy for temporary pleasures?
4. What caused you to see the falseness of the world and the end of it?
5. What are some commandments that have seemed oppressing to you?
6. What are some man-made commandments that we have seen required of Christians? How could these become oppressing?

Chapter Nine
bowling pins and archery targets

> I have endeavored to read the Scriptures as though no one had read them before me, and I am as much on my guard against reading them today through my views yesterday as I am against being influenced by any foreign name, authority, or system whatever.
>
> —Alexander Campbell

The great leader of the American Restoration Movement challenged the people of his day to go back to the Bible. He wanted them to take a fresh look at the scriptures as if they had never seen them before. He hoped that people could examine the Word without the blinders of traditions and creeds that had prejudiced their viewpoints. It was a difficult quest, but it was a good one. I think that it's still a good plea. It's where I've wanted to be in my own study of the Bible. But even if you have come from a heritage that emphasizes getting back to the Bible and the Bible only, it's still a very difficult task to do.

I have often wished that I could strip away the biases, prejudices, and viewpoints that I carry around with me and look at the Bible without reading something into it. Wouldn't it be nice if we could keep from biasing ourselves even by our own prejudices? Although it's difficult, and we will never be able to rid ourselves of the way we color our interpretation, it still is a noble task to keep seeking afresh the message of God's Word.

In one of those classified ads of a religious journal, I once observed an advertisement of a church looking for a new preacher. Two humorous qualifications were given. They were looking for a man who didn't know Greek and hadn't been to the Holy Land. No telling how many church members have been bored by dull word studies and boring slides of the Near East. In spite of that, I would like us to consider the meaning of a particular word used in the Bible. On one of those days when I was needing to rethink my faith, the study of a certain word led me to a perplexing question.

Not counting *agape*, the word for love, the first Greek word that I remember learning was the word for "sin." It's *hamartia*. I was told that this word literally means to miss the mark. And that's still a pretty good definition. The illustration given me was of an archer aiming at a target. If his arrow missed the target, it is as if he had sinned. Another way to look at it would be a pitcher in baseball who is aiming at the catcher's mitt. To sin would be to miss the target, the catcher's glove. I remember such an incident well. It was another opening day for the Mariners. This time it was on the road. Again I was excited with the thrill of a new season. There was hope for the first game since our ex-ace, Mark Langston, was on the mound. As he wound up to throw that first pitch, I once again had visions of glory for my lowly team. But at the moment of his delivery, he lost his grip and the ball went sailing over the catcher's hand, over the umpire's head, and landed high on the backstop protecting the fans. It was a fitting beginning for another season. He had sinned. He had missed the mark. The target was in the right place, but he simply missed it.

The same is true with our spiritual sin. God has given us His law. Many aim at it, others don't. But even the people who take great pains to hit the intended target often wildly miss the ultimate goal. As Paul clearly stated: "all have sinned and fall short of the glory of God" (Romans 3:23).

Missing the mark was an easy concept for me to understand. However, it was the concept that was the opposite of hitting the mark that brought me great confusion. Let me explain to you how this came about.

In a class on missions at Abilene Christian University, Wendell Broom, my instructor, asked us a most intriguing question. It had to do with bowling and archery, two sports that are not my greatest interests. His question was this: "Are God's commandments more like bowling pins or an archery target?"

At first his question did not make a lot of sense to me. But the key to this point was in the differences of the scorekeeping. In bowling all the pins are worth the same amount. In other words if you knock over the ten pin or the three pin, you are still only awarded one on your score. All the pins in bowling are worth the same amount.

However, it is quite different in archery. If you hit the target, some areas are worth more than others. When the arrow hits the bullseye, you score many more points than when you hit one of the fringe circles on the periphery of the target.

So again, "Are God's commandments more like bowling pins or an archery target?" In other words, are all of God's commandments of the same importance or are some more important than others?

My response was, "They are like bowling pins. They are all of the same importance." My reasoning was that any sin whether lying or murder was enough to make you miss the mark. No matter what sin (whether it appeared great or small) you committed, it was enough to make you imperfect and need salvation. Any sin or any number of sins could damn you equally. Once we sin we are all equally lost and in need of a Savior. Therefore, it seemed to me that if sin is equal, then obedience would also be.

But my teacher said, "No, you are wrong. God's commandments are like an archery target." He was telling me that some commandments are more important than others. Could this be true? It was certainly not what I thought or had been taught. The only way I was going to be able to deal with this was to do what was suggested at the first of this chapter – look at the Word afresh without my preconceived ideas. My biggest concern was that if I pursued this honestly and I differed with my present conviction, where would it lead me? Would I be willing to examine the Bible in such a way that I would go where it led me even if it was different from where I had been for years? It was a scary thought. Although it seemed like this particular question of the weight of some commandments compared to others wasn't that significant, actually it had been at the heart of what had caused many divisions in history.

Going back to the target illustration, I had to wrestle with another question. If it was sin to miss the target, then what would it be to hit the bullseye? Because if God's commandments were not of equal value, could it be possible that I had been content with merely landing a few arrows on the target instead of hitting the bullseye? Or is it even possible that my aim was never at the bullseye? Could I have been aiming at the wrong part of the target? Is it possible that my arrows were always on the peripheral edge of the target because that is where I took aim? It's not that I had not tried to obey God's commandments. Rather it's that I had aimed at some that don't count as much while never hitting the bullseye. And scariest of all – would I know the bullseye if I hit it?

This was radical thinking to me. Maybe it is to you also. Possibly you don't agree yet that commands are weighted differently. But after an examination, I think my professor was correct. Anyhow, it certainly bears looking at.

As I have stated, I had always believed that God's commands were weighted equally. It was like the commands were all on level ground with none of them higher than another. I had never considered that they could be like a stairstep with some of them loftier than others.

Would this mean then that you don't have to obey the lesser important commandments? No, that's not the point. That would take us back to meriting our honor before God. It would be a return to that philosophy of finding what I don't have to do and still be acceptable to God. That's legalism again. We should strive to obey all of God's commandments, but some are more important than others.

It's mainly a matter of focus that we are trying to reconsider. Because it is possible that we have focused on certain commandments while rejecting others. Unless we are perfect, all of us have done this. Then, which commandments have we neglected and which ones have we kept? Which ones have been our focus and which ones have received less attention?

Our tendency when we weigh commandments equally is to think that we focus on them all equally. That simply is not true. Any preacher who would examine all of his sermons of the last year would discover that not all of God's commandments got equal billing and emphasis. So which ones won out? And are they the same ones that God would want emphasized at the expense of keeping others in the background?

It is also possible that one could keep one commandment and violate another in the process of keeping the first one. This could be especially devastating if the one violated was more important than the one kept. How would this be possible?

In my church history, it seemed to me that all commandments were of equal value. Since much of the focus of restorationism has been in finding the exact model for the organization of the church, God's teaching in this area has been considered to be very important. And certainly we want to be the kind of church God wants us to be. But what if in an attempt to keep a doctrine on organization, an attitude prevailed which was not the disposition that Christ wanted? What if in the obeying of the organizational doctrine, the disposition of Christ was not kept? What should have been done? Obviously, the doctrine of the organization and the character of Christ should have both been obeyed. But which one was most important?

We all know that we are going to miss some of the demands of character prescribed in the Bible. And most of us are pretty lenient when it comes to missing the mark here. Why is there not that same graciousness when it comes to someone who misses the mark on a doctrine other than disposition? And why is it that our disposition is usually so bad when someone doesn't see how they missed the doctrine? And what's most important?

Jerry Jones challenged my thinking immensely when he said, "I'd rather miss a doctrine of Christ than the disposition of Christ. If I miss a doctrine, I might do it by ignorance. But if I miss His disposition, I always do it by choice." He elaborated that he wanted to obey all that God commanded, but most of all, he wanted to have that character of Christ.

When it comes to my religious arguments in the past, too often I was correct in a doctrine and wrong in my disposition. And I was trying to convert someone who was incorrect in a particular doctrine but was possessing the character of Christ in the process. Could he have seen my position if I had a different character? Perhaps I was the one most in need of a conversion.

If some of God's commands are more important than others, it is of necessity that I find the ones of greatest value and make them my focus. Does this mean the others have no value? During recent years, you have probably noticed little containers by cash registers in stores which are full of pennies. There's usually a sign that says "Take one/give one." Their purpose is to keep you from having to break a larger bill or coin. People today are easily willing to give or take a penny. The same would not be true of ten dollar bills. Does that mean pennies have no value? No, if they had no value, they would be discarded. They have value and still are counted. But their value is not as great as our other currency. We shouldn't discard commandments that are of lesser value. They still should be counted. But we still must be in search of and focus on the ones of greatest value.

Questions for Discussion

1. Why is it difficult for you to take a fresh look at the Scriptures?
2. What influences color your interpretation of the Bible?
3. What areas of your belief are most difficult to honestly examine?
4. Explain what "sin" is. Where do you find yourself most often missing the mark?
5. How would you have answered the question, "Are God's commandments like bowling pins or an archery target?" Why?
6. Do you usually find yourself aiming at the bullseye or the edge of the target in your religion? Explain.
7. Are you lacking more in what is usually called "doctrine" or a proper disposition? Give an example.

Chapter Ten
hitting the bullseye with our doctrine

Sound doctrine. Those two words conjure up some very negative feelings within me. And not to my surprise, I've found that many others react the same way. Recently a group of us were going to a minister's seminar when someone asked, "What's the subject?"

"Sound doctrine," was the reply.

"Oh, no!" three others responded in unison.

Was this a group of wild-eyed liberals who didn't respect the authority of Scriptures? No, not at all. They were simply recalling how they had all been burned in the past by someone else's quest for "sound doctrine."

Sound doctrine could literally be translated

"healthy teaching." But what has often been heralded as the tenets of sound doctrine have been anything but healthy to the lives of many Christians and churches. What was called healthy brought back memories of hurt and division. In my experience, sound doctrine was being on the right side of whatever issue was being debated at the moment. Therefore, sound doctrine from my perspective had been the possession of the right arguments on baptism, instrumental music in worship, divorce and remarriage, church cooperation, discipling, versions of the Bible, and other issues. Are these important? Some are and some aren't. Are they biblical doctrines? Some are, and others are issues not even mentioned in the Bible.

What bothers me is that in our study of doctrine, we usually only consider those aspects that are impersonal rather than the qualities of character (or what was called "disposition" in the last chapter). Aren't these personal marks of character also a part of our doctrine? Could it be possible that they are just as important if not more important than the other doctrinal issues we discuss?

When Paul writes to Titus and exhorts "But as for you, speak the things which are fitting for sound doctrine" (Titus 2:1), what comes to your mind as "sound doctrine"? Usually we interpret it to mean those particular beliefs that distinguish us as New Testament Christians. However in the context of this passage, the sound doctrine also refers to elements that mark the character of older men, older women, young men, and bondslaves.

For example, Paul describes a healthy older man as one who is "temperate, dignified, sensible, sound in faith, in love, in perseverance." To Paul a man's character was certainly an enormous part of his doctrine.

When the law expert comes to test Jesus in Matthew 22, he asks, "Teacher, which is the greatest commandment in the Law?"

Obviously, Jesus could have listed hundreds of commandments from the Law which God had revealed. He could have said that they were all just as important. But instead, He singles out two commandments and ranks them as the most important.

First of all, Jesus told him, " 'Love the Lord your God with all your heart and with all your soul and with all your mind,' This is the first and greatest commandment" (v. 37-38). To Jesus there was nothing more important than this one commandment. No other was its equal.

Secondly, Jesus told him, "Love your neighbor as yourself." He then went on to explain that all the other commandments hinge on the first two that are the most important.

Paul echoes this same teaching in his letter to the Romans. "Let no debt remain outstanding, except the continuing debt to love one another, for he who loves his fellowman has fulfilled the law. The commandments, 'Do not commit adultery,' 'Do not murder,' 'Do not steal,' 'Do not covet,' and whatever other commandment there may be, are summed up in this one rule: 'Love your neighbor as yourself.' Love does no harm to its neighbor. Therefore love is the fulfillment of the law" (Romans 13:8-10).

An examination of Jesus and Paul would tell us that we could do all the details of the law and be as meticulous as possible, but if we fail to love, we miss the bullseye. If sin is missing the target, what's hitting the bullseye? Jesus pinpoints it. It's loving God and loving people.

Jesus' teaching still holds true today. The problem is that a lot of us focus on many things that are religious, churchy, and even biblical but miss love. It's not that we totally miss the target. Rather, it's that we are too often missing the bullseye. An equally perplexing problem is when we aim at the periphery of the target rather than the bullseye. Far too often, churches have been most concerned with the details, and as a result, missed loving God and people.

I'll never forget my early conversations with a young co-ed who was later to become my wife. I was a campus minister and Barbie had come to me to argue some doctrinal differences that tended to separate our churches. At best our difference was on the periphery of Jesus' target. However, the place on the target does not minimize an intensity for belief or an inability to argue. Using every argument that I could think of, I tried to persuade Barbie where she was wrong. I read books which proposed every argument on this particular issue. But with all my logic and persuasion, she remained unconvinced.

What was I to do? I figured that there had to be one more argument which I had failed to articulate. There had to be one bit of reason that upon hearing it, everything would click and then she would think just like me. In search of that final apologetic, I made an appointment to talk to Dr. Furman Kearley who was the head of the Bible department at Lubbock Christian College. If anyone would know the missing ingredient, I thought it would be him since he probably knew more of the Bible than anyone else in town.

After telling Dr. Kearley all of the arguments, I had used, I asked, "Are those correct?"

"Yes" he said, "your reasoning is correct and biblical."

"Well, can you give another argument that I can use on her?" I pleaded.

"No. I don't know of any others," he responded.

"You mean that's all there is?"

"Yes, those are all the arguments that I know on that issue," he told me.

"Then what am I going to do?" I inquired dejectedly.

"I guess you'll just have to love her," he said.

So I did. Little did we know how much I would love her.

Later, Barbie changed her thinking. Even she agreed that I was right in my positions. I asked her what had persuaded her to see things differently. Needless to say, it wasn't one of my great arguments. She said that it was the love of all the students in the campus ministry. She had never been with people who loved God and loved her so much. It was through the eyes of love that she perceived the truth about the other issue.

Most of our divisions among Christians and congregations have occurred because we have focused on the edge of the target rather than on the bullseye. In fact, it would be difficult to prove that some of our issues were even on the target at all. What becomes a disaster is that in the midst of all of our arguments on these issues, we miss what is most important – we forget to love. We miss the center of the target because the edge has become more important than the bullseye.

After being asked upon an occasion to speak on the subject of discipleship, I was told that I had to meet a certain criteria before I could address the seminar. Before I could speak on discipleship, the elders at a church participating in the seminar wanted to make sure that I agreed with a man in Tennessee on his view of divorce and remarriage and not with a man in Arkansas. To tell you the truth, I had not read what either one of these men had written on the subject. The people already had in writing what I was to say on discipleship and the issue of divorce and remarriage was not even a topic at the seminar. Yet, unless I met their standard on this issue, I wouldn't get to speak. Certainly, this is focusing on the periphery. Everything in Christianity could only be seen through the issue of divorce and remarriage to these men. And in the process of their screening for soundness, they had most definitely forgotten

HITTING THE BULLSEYE WITH OUR DOCTRINE

to love me. When it came to their relationship with people, they had missed the bullseye.

When I examine most of the church divisions that have occurred in my heritage, it is obvious that we did not divide over the bullseye. Major divisions have occurred over instrumental music in worship, churches cooperating in orphan homes, even the number of cups at the Lord's Supper. These issues are peripheral at best.

I appreciated what Jerry Jones once said in a sermon that I heard. He said, "The problem is that we read the Bible looking for facts or as a debater's handbook. We want to argue about issues instead of knowing Jesus and being conformed to Him." There's such a great truth to that statement. Instead of opening our hearts and minds up to the central truth that God is revealing – a salvation through Jesus – we often start with our issues and go to the Bible to back up our arguments.

My conviction is this – until you understand the most important doctrines, the others will not become clear. In other words, the peripheral issues should only be dealt with through the eyes of a love for God and man.

When we are approaching people who differ with us on issues of religion, we usually start debating on how we disagree. Wouldn't it be better if we started our relationship with a commitment to love each other? If both of us had a mutual love for God and his commandments, shouldn't that be first of all affirmed and appreciated? The way to have unity is to focus on the bullseye. We probably would have never divided over peripheral issues if the commitment to love God and each other was always in the forefront of a relationship. In fact, most divisions occur when in the process of the argument, love is lost. It's probably the lack of love which causes most divisions more than an initial disagreement on peripheral issues.

There was an early plea in the Restoration movement. It was something like this:

In matters of faith – unity.

In matters of opinion – liberality.

In all matters – charity.

The early Restoration movement was characterized by people uniting. In latter times, it has been characterized by people dividing. Could it be that love has not been shown?

A good friend of mine terminated his ministry of preaching at a church recently because of the concerns of his elders. They wrote to him, "We knew when you came here that you preached on liberty, love and grace. However, we thought that you would grow out of it." Can you believe it? I know that attitude exists, but it was so shocking to actually behold it in print. They had hoped that he would lose his focus on liberty, love, and grace and be more concerned with their particular issues. If he were to grow out of liberty, love, and grace; what was he to grow into – slavery, hate, and legalism? Surely, that's not what they had in mind, but a wrong focus can lead us into some pretty scary places.

HITTING THE BULLSEYE WITH OUR DOCTRINE

Questions for Discussion

1. What do you first think of when someone mentions "sound doctrine"?
2. Has what has been called "sound doctrine" always been healthy for you?
3. When you discuss doctrine do you only discuss the impersonal aspects, or do you also talk about personal character? Explain.
4. What are some peripheral areas that have often been the focus of your faith?
5. How have we won many of our debates and still not brought unity?
6. How can we focus on the bullseye with people who differ from us?
7. Have the arrows been landing near the bullseye or the edge of the target in your own faith? Give some examples.

Chapter Eleven
hitting the bullseye in our lifestyle

Have you ever been sitting in church on Sunday morning thinking, "I hate this assembly"? What caused that feeling of frustration? Was everything just so boring? Did the songleader pick out all the wrong songs? Was the sermon too long? You've been there before, haven't you?

Wouldn't it be interesting to see the assembly from God's point of view? Don't you wonder if He's not looking down on that church meeting shaking His head and saying – "I hate this assembly"? What would make Him want to say something like that? Would it be that we got the order of things all wrong? It should have been two songs before the prayer. Probably not. Could it be that the form wasn't exact enough? Certainly God is concerned about form, but that isn't his only priority. Or is it that the hearts of the people were wrong as they were going through the forms? That's getting very close to God's great desire for us, but there is one specific time that God said "I hate this assembly." What was the reason?

The occasion is found in the prophecy of Amos "I hate, I despise your religious feasts; I cannot stand your assemblies. Even though you bring me burnt offerings and grain offerings, I will not accept them. Though you bring choice fellowship offerings, I will have no regard for them. Away with the noise of your songs! I will not listen to the music of your harps" (Amos 5:21-23). In this passage, God tells the people of Israel that He hates their assemblies. He further states that He doesn't want their sacrifices and offerings. Even their songs and music are not pleasing anymore to the Almighty. What happened? The key is found in what God did want – "But let justice roll on like a river, righteousness like a never-failing stream!" (Amos 5:24). The people had kept their forms of worship, but when they were not in their assemblies, they treated people unjustly. Therefore, God could no longer stand their assemblies. When we assemble today, God hates our assemblies if during the week we have not been concerned about the injustices and inequities of the world. Our lifestyle in the world is of utmost importance to God.

Again Isaiah reiterates how the lack of a just

and holy lifestyle can completely negate one's personal or corporate worship. "Stop bringing meaningless offerings! Your incense is detestable to me. New Moons, Sabbaths and convocations – I cannot bear your evil assemblies. Your New Moon festivals and your appointed feasts my soul hates. They have become a burden to me; I am weary of bearing them. When you spread out your hands in prayer, I will hide my eyes from you; even if you offer many prayers, I will not listen. Your hands are full of blood; wash and make yourselves clean. Take your evil deeds out of my sight! Stop doing wrong, learn to do right! Seek justice, encourage the oppressed. Defend the cause of the fatherless, plead the case of the widow" (Isaiah 1:13-17).

In our conversations and debates on worship, most concerns have centered around form and content. Truly these are important and vital, but without a proper lifestyle, they are meaningless.

Skid Road is a most famous street in Seattle. Years ago, loggers would cut down trees at the top of one of Seattle's great hills and skid these logs down to the bay where they could be transported for lumber. This road that the timber traveled down became known as Skid Road. Over the years, many of the down-and-outers gathered at the bottom of Skid Road, and thus the title "Skid Road bums" was born. Now all over the country, areas where the homeless and destitute gather are called "Skid Row."

One day the Peanut Butter brigade invaded Skid Road. I had taken a bunch of college students down to distribute food among the homeless and hungry of Seattle. Walking down 1st Avenue in the Skid Road area, we handed out hundreds of peanut butter sandwiches. As we gave away the sandwiches, we also invited people to come to a mission for a hot meal that evening where they could also hear about the Good News. A middle aged man shuffling up the street with his head down was now within distance of my invitation. After taking a sandwich and listening to my spiel, he looked up and said, "Milton Jones, you are the last person I expected to see on First Avenue."

Recently a local news radio station was interviewing an author who had written a book on where Jesus would go if he were to come back today. Listeners were invited to call and respond to him telling where they thought Jesus would be if he were in Seattle today. Nearly every caller agreed that if Jesus were to come to Seattle today, he would be down on First Avenue near Skid Road.

After hearing this broadcast, I asked myself why was it that I was the last person someone in need expected to see on First Avenue when it was the first place people expected Jesus to be. It was an indicting encounter that told me a lot about our faith. Many church members have reached the point where the world doesn't even expect them to be like Jesus or have his priorities. It's like they forgot what really counts.

What do churches count? We keep track of attendance, contributions, baptisms, and other pertinent statistics. Often we keep track of these vital statistics as if they were the measuring rod for entrance into the pearly gates on judgment day. But no statistical measure merits entrance into the kingdom of heaven. On the other hand, it is interesting to note what Jesus will count on judgment day.

> When the Son of Man comes in his glory, and all the angels with him, he will sit on his throne in heavenly glory. All the nations will be gathered before him, and he will separate the people one from another as a shepherd separates the sheep from the goats. He will put the sheep on his right, and the goats on his left. Then the King will say to those on his right. "Come, you who are blessed by my Father; take your inheritance, the kingdom prepared for you since the creation of the world. For I was hungry and you gave me something to eat, I was thirsty and you gave me something to drink, I was a stranger and you invited me in, I needed clothes and you clothed me, I was sick and you looked after me, I was in prison and you came to visit me." Then the righteous will answer him, "Lord, when did we see you hungry and feed you, or thirsty and give you something to drink? When did we see you a stranger and invite you in, or needing clothes and clothe you? When did we see you sick or in prison and go to visit you?" The King will reply, "I tell you the truth, whatever you did for one of the least of these brothers of mine, you did for me." Then he will say to those on his left, "Depart from me, you who are cursed, into the eternal fire prepared for the devil and his angels. For I was hungry and you gave me nothing to eat, I was thirsty and you gave me nothing to drink, I was a stranger and you did not invite me in, I needed clothes and you did not clothe me, I was sick and in prison and you did not look after me."

They also will answer, "Lord, when did we see you hungry or thirsty or a stranger or needing clothes or sick or in prison, and did not help you?" He will reply, "I tell you the truth, whatever you did not do for one of the least of these, you did not do for me." Then they will go away to eternal punishment, but the righteous to eternal life (Matt. 25:31-46).

Was Jesus kidding here or was he serious? It's easy to take this as some kind of an allegory and excuse ourselves from helping the downtrodden. But in all actuality, Jesus meant what he said here. God cares whether or not we care. Helping needy people counts with God. Hitting the bullseye in our lifestyle is critical in our faith. When it comes to what we do, some things are more important than others. Maybe no other passage demonstrates this better than Matthew 23:23, "Woe to you teachers of the law and Pharisees, you hypocrites! You give a tenth of your spices—mint, dill and cummin. But you have neglected the more important matters of the law—justice, mercy and faithfulness. You should have practiced the latter, without neglecting the former."

The Pharisees are branded as hypocrites here even though they were meticulous in obedience. They had taken great pains in the details of their law keeping. The issue here was tithing. Should they have tithed? Yes; however, people generally tithed from their main crops. It appears that this group of Pharisees were so detailed that they now were measuring the most minute of their garden plants.

HITTING THE BULLSEYE IN OUR LIFESTYLE

What was the problem? Again, they had dwelled on the peripheral elements of their religion and missed the bullseye. Jesus told them that some things were weightier than weighing out a tenth of their garden plants. Justice, mercy and faithfulness are weightier than the details of their tithe.

Jesus was telling the religious people of His day not to simply play religion. He's still telling us that today. We can't just go to church, keep the rules of the church, and not let it affect our lifestyle. He tells us that there are some matters that are more important than the rules on which we often concentrate—things like justice, mercy, and faithfulness.

Our religion is not focused, however many rules we keep, if we are not concerned about justice. In a world full of racial prejudice, starving children, and violent crime, we cannot turn a deaf ear to the cries of injustice and then pretend that we walk in the steps of the Lord. When people are treated with inequity, it is no small matter to Jesus. He says it is weighty. We cannot let it slip away from our focus.

In a society where everyone is looking out for number one, mercy is often a lost commodity. But not so with Jesus. With the rise of AIDS, homelessness, divorces and the other complex problems of our age, mercy is desperately needed. Our dog-eat-dog world has left people with a sense of loneliness and hopelessness. The kind word, the helpful deed in a cold, heartless world is at the heart of our Christianity.

Each year I survey people to find the greatest need in our community and then address it in a sermon on our "Bring Your Neighbor" day. Last year the overall concern in our neighborhood was the sense of a lack of integrity in nearly every aspect of our society. It was seen in politics, sports, entertainment, and even in religion. A lack of integrity is displayed when people break their promises and don't keep their commitments. It's a lack of character that is manifested when you can no longer count on a person's word. This failure in today's society is just the opposite of what Jesus called faithfulness. Jesus calls us to have a stick-to-it-tiveness that is seen in our perseverance and heard in our "yes being yes." This faithfulness so absent from our culture is at the heart of what's important to Jesus.

Justice, mercy, and faithfulness are weighty matters to the one who follows Christ. Our doctrine should change our lives and not simply be words we talk about. In the early days of Christianity, faith was something that was lived out in the streets. As it became legalized and more acceptable, it became for many something that was only talked about in the houses of worship.

Our doctrine today should also change our lives and not simply be something we talk about. In verse 24, Jesus says "You blind guides! You strain out a gnat but swallow a camel." In a humorous way, Jesus depicts a scene of one of the Pharisees trying to be pure and undefiled. He strains a liquid through gauze to avoid drinking a gnat. In his detail, Jesus declares that he swallows a camel which would also be unclean. His humor points out how absurd we often are in the practice of our religion. It is as if we completely lose our common sense when it comes to figuring out what is important.

It is easy for us to dwell on all the hot issues of religion and not change our lifestyle. Our religion becomes more what we talk about than how we live. You can miss the bullseye even if you are right on the periphery. You will not grow as a church or as an individual if you are aiming at the periphery, even if you are correct about the periphery. We must focus on the bullseye — the periphery is simply not as important.

Jesus speaks of some issues that are toward the center of the target—he calls them weightier. They are aspects of our lives that show whether or not we care.

Recently we had a series in our home Bible study groups that proved to be very relevant. People said that the subject hit them where they lived. The studies were based on a cliche that I first heard from Charles Colson of Watergate fame. He was standing in line at a car rental agency. The man in front of him was irate over the unavailability of a certain make of car. Angrily the man screamed, "I must have a black Lincoln Continental!" The attendant offered him other cars and even a white Lincoln Continental at a reduced price. The man was obstinate. He would accept nothing less than a black Lincoln Continental.

When she asked him why, he said, "Because I am going to a party where everyone else will be in black Lincoln Continentals and I must be in one too." Appalled at the man's behavior, Colson finally figured the man out when he saw his world view written on the front of his teeshirt. It said, "The one with the most toys when he dies wins."

This materialistic, grab-all-you-can-get mentality has captured our society.

Jesus' weightier matters are strikingly different from what the world deems important. Jesus focuses not on what we can get but rather on what we can compassionately give.

Jesus is calling our world to be turned upside down. He's telling us that we have our world view backwards. We love things and use people when we should love people and use things. Even when we invite people to church, we say "we could really use you here." Why don't we invite people by saying "we could really love you here."

While waiting in the airport in San Francisco, I noticed a wildly dressed, nervous, and generally "out of place" man in the terminal. As I got near him, I wondered how long it had been since he had bathed. Only one thing crossed my mind as I boarded the plane to go to Southern California – I hoped that I didn't have to sit by this man. After all, I had to work on an important message that I was about to deliver. You've guessed the end of the story, haven't you? My seat was directly beside you-know-who. To make matters worse, he was a talker, and he didn't know English very well. After a while, he opened his briefcase and showed me pictures of over a hundred orphans whom he took care of in Haiti. He told me how he tried to feed them and teach them of Jesus. A church had asked him to come to the United States and tell of the hunger problem in Haiti, and he had agreed since they promised a few hundred dollars to help with his work. Before I left that man, he had my money, and he's still getting it.

The man from Haiti taught me an important lesson that day. He helped me to see how I had missed the weightier matters. Appearance, money, and my religious agenda had skewed my perception of what was important. Justice and mercy in my lifestyle had been put on the back burner in preference for my talk about faith.

We shy away from mercy and benevolence today because we are afraid that we might get burned. Because of the rip-off artists in the world, we are concerned that someone is going to take advantage of us. We hold back our gifts because a person might not be deserving. Aren't you glad God doesn't withhold His gifts when we take advantage of Him and are less than deserving? He keeps on giving when we abuse His gifts and are certainly less than honest. The gift is grace. Nothing is more important to us than to receive the gift we don't deserve. And the response to grace is to be gracious. And nothing becomes more important in our faith than to give the gift and help those who are equally undeserving.

Questions For Discussion

1. Have you ever thought, "I hate this assembly"? How might God's viewpoint differ from your own?
2. Would it be surprising to see you among the downtrodden in your city? Where do you think Jesus would be if he came to your town?
3. What do you usually count in your church? If you counted what Jesus mentions in Matthew 25, how would you be doing?
4. What are the weightier matters Jesus mentions in Matthew 23:23? Which of these needs to be weightier in your lifestyle? Give some examples.
5. Where have you strained gnats and swallowed camels?
6. How have you loved things and used people in your life? How could you change?
7. Have you ever held back your helping because you thought someone was taking advantage of you? How could you have a more gracious approach to benevolence?

Chapter Twelve
hitting the bullseye with our message

A new profanity has emerged in some churches. A profanity is one of those words that you are not supposed to say. This time it's not a four letter word. In fact it used to be one of our most important words. It's "evangelism." I discovered this one day when I was asked to preach at a church. They told me that I could speak on "anything but evangelism." Maybe other churches would not put it as bluntly, but talk about sharing the good news to our world has definitely subsided in many churches. Haven't you noticed a lack of evangelism in churches today? It's interesting to note the evolution of many seminars that were born out of a concern for soul winning. Now it's difficult to even find the subject of evangelism being addressed at some of them. I've also noticed something about the crowds at the seminars recently. When the people leave the meetings, I hear talk about how impressed they were with the speakers. In times past, they left motivated to do something about the mission. Our churches are disturbingly being filled with observers rather than participants. What happened?

When it comes to evangelism, we have become disillusioned. To help us understand what happened, we need to examine several aspects of ministry. When I first got involved in campus ministry, I was given a book to read. Being the first religious book that I had read outside the Bible, it helped shape my philosophy of ministry. The book, *The Witness* by Urie Bender, described ministry with the use of four M's - mission, message, motivation, and method. His proposition was that all four of these areas must be examined for the ministry to work properly. As a result, when we see a disillusionment with the mission or evangelism, we will also see negative interrelationships with these other aspects of ministry.

Our disillusionment with the mission was closely connected to a disillusionment that existed with our message. In many circles, the message had become the church. We were telling the world that we had the right kind of church. That was our message. In fact, for many, all they knew how to do in evangelism was simply to invite people to the church. But some of us got disillusioned with the church. Our disillusionments came for varying reasons. Some said that the church had become too liberal, while others said it was too legalistic. But for whatever reason, people had become disillusioned with the church that they saw. It might be said that the church had a bad self image. We had doubts about ourselves, and we had become the message. Because of our negative self concept, it looked like we had bad news rather than good news to communicate to the lost. As a result, we quit talking to the world. Our problems became overwhelming to us because indeed there were many. And the assumption was made that we had to straighten ourselves out first before we could speak to the world. But when does that happen? The longer we focused on ourselves, the more problems we discovered.

Our disillusionment over the mission also was intimately connected with our disillusionment with our motivation. As we examined ourselves, we discovered that we weren't always being evangelistic for the right reasons. There had been an overconcern with numbers. Too many converts had become statistics rather than people who were loved unconditionally. Churches began to be evaluated by whether or not they made the lists of the fastest growing churches. Church leaders felt inadequate if they failed to appear on such lists. Others were deemed successful simply because they made the list. Leadership became to some people how many notches a person had on his evangelistic belt. In order to get a greater performance and improve the bottom line, leaders would lay great guilt trips on the people to keep the numbers up. And as a result, Christians began to feel that their salvation was tied into their personal evangelism. As God's grace was discovered and the improper motivation in evangelism realized – it's no wonder there was disillusionment.

A greater examination of God's grace also produced a disillusionment with many of our methods. With an honest evaluation, we learned that many of our approaches were trying to manipulate people into the kingdom by trickery and sales techniques. We approached people with hidden agendas and hoops to jump through whether they were questions to answer that upon completion would make them arrive at our conclusion, or activities planned that would slowly and cautiously hook them until the time came that they agreed with us. But our lack of being upfront with people and the basic dishonesty of some of our approaches left many feeling empty. The methods too often led only to guilt and not to grace.

If the mission of Jesus is still valid, and it is, our disillusionment must be overcome. To deal with the mission, these other areas must be explored. As already mentioned in chapter seven, our motivation in evangelism needs to be rooted in grace rather than guilt or legalism. Our methods, also, must be honest and above reproach. But our greatest change must come in a realization of what needs to be the focus of our message. For an evangelistic zeal to be renewed in our churches, we must be hitting the bullseye with our message. We must look at what we are talking about.

Paul makes it clear in I Corinthians 15:1-4 what the bullseye is in our message. "Now I make known to you, brethren, the gospel which I preached to you, which also you received, in which also you stand, by which also you are saved, if you hold fast the word which I preached to you, unless you believed in vain. For I delivered to you as of first importance what I also received, that Christ died for our sins according to the Scriptures, and that He was buried, and that He was raised on the third day according to Scriptures." For Paul, the gospel is the message of utmost importance. It's the story of the death, burial and resurrection of Jesus that is to take preeminence in our talk. This is it. No message is more important. Our emphasis should be clear. Our message must focus on Jesus. When it doesn't, we miss the mark.

As Christians, we may differ in our opinions on many issues. But when it comes to the gospel, this is the bottom line. There is no flexibility. There is no message more central and crucial to our cause than the story of Jesus.

The gospel message is not only central to our faith, but it is also the core that we can hang on to when we start getting mixed up on all of the other issues. In anyone's honest examination of the Christian system, there will be times of doubts, frustrations, and indecision. What can you hold on to during those times to keep you from forsaking it all? I remember times in my own spiritual journey when I was around circles of people who caused me to question the correctness of not only their position on issues but also my own. I've been in some groups that missed the point through their legalism. I knew something was wrong, but at first, I couldn't put my finger on the problem. It was a focus on the central message of Jesus that finally helped me see what was wrong and gave me perseverance when in the midst of a group that was wrong. On other occasions, I have been mixed up by some who took a more liberal position on the Word and became lax where it certainly seemed God had some strong standards. But at the time, I couldn't quite see the proper position. Again it was a focus on the core of the message of Christ that kept me from being disillusioned or going outside the boundaries I now believe that God has set for me. A missionary friend of mine told me of his experiences in a foreign land. In his work, he became mixed up on exactly what constituted the pattern of the church. Instead of quitting because he had questions about certain aspects of the church, he focused his sermons on that which was positive – the gospel of Jesus. The result was that people heard his message of Jesus more than any message before and people were converted to the Christ. The church grew, and he learned what was the true essence of the church – it is the people who have believed and responded to that message of the gospel.

Too often we have been mixed up on what's most important in our message. A lady left the church where I was preaching and gave as her reason that I didn't preach the gospel. The irony of it was that I had been preaching verse by verse through the gospel of John for over a year. She did not recognize the death, burial, and resurrection as the gospel. Instead she said that sermons should have as their emphasis the five steps to salvation. This was the core of the gospel according to her.

It was in the early 1800's that Walter Scott traversed Ohio on horseback. Scott taught his "Plan of Salvation" using his famous "five-finger exercise." The illustrative preacher would ride into town on his horse and gather around him all the children he could find. He would then say, "Hold up your left hands and repeat after me." Then, he would let each one of his fingers represent a step in the plan of salvation: faith, repentance, baptism, remission of sins, and the gift of the Holy Spirit. After the kids memorized these steps, Scott would send them home to repeat the five-finger illustration to their parents and tell them that Scott would be speaking on this subject at a meeting in a nearby schoolhouse.

It was a good illustration. It was an effective way to get people to a meeting. But the five-finger illustration Scott taught the children isn't the gospel itself. Certainly these five points are important doctrines in our Christianity, and they should decidedly be expounded. However, to say that if they are omitted in a sermon or not done like Scott did then the gospel isn't being preached is going too far. This is especially true if in the sermon the gospel as Paul defined it – the death, burial, and resurrection of Jesus – has indeed been emphasized.

Maybe what bothers me most about Scott's illustration is that somewhere along the way, many churches changed the steps. In Scott's illustration the fingers represented faith, repentance, baptism, remission of sins, and the gift of the Holy Spirit. That's not the way I learned it. The steps that were taught me were hear, believe, repent, confess, and be baptized. What's the difference? The new version only emphasizes what man does and completely eliminates what God gives in the process – remission of sins and the gift of the Holy Spirit. Again we have discovered right in the heart of what has become a central part of our message a lack of emphasis on God's grace. The emphasis has become what man must do to be saved rather than what God has done (the death, burial and resurrection of Jesus) and will do (forgive our sins and give us the Holy Spirit). We will never hit the bullseye in our message until our emphasis is upon God's work rather than our own.

Church bulletin typos are always humorous to me. One of my favorites was in a bulletin from a church in Canada. Instead of reading "Church of Christ," the bulletin heading said "Church or Christ." It was like you had a choice – do you choose the church or do you choose Christ? But when it comes to our message, often we do make a choice between these two. I believe in both, but what is our emphasis in preaching and what is of first importance? It has dawned on me that our message to the world and the church has focused extensively on the church rather than the Christ. As I examined our evangelistic approaches to lead people to conversion, the emphasis of most of them has been to convert people to the right kind of church rather than to Jesus as Lord. A greater emphasis on the church rather than the Christ has also been reflected in our preaching. It's scary to think that we might be spending more time trying to get people to convert to us rather than to Jesus.

Our emphasis must be the Christ. He must be lifted up in our message as of first importance. Paul said "we preach Christ and Him crucified." What has been your focus? If you don't know, ask the people who listen to you. Ask them "Do I talk more about the church or about Jesus?"

When I went to the University of Washington to start a campus ministry, I began a Bible study in one of the dorms. Every one of my studies in that first group began with this statement: "I believe that Jesus Christ is the most amazing man to ever walk on the face of the earth. I don't know what you think of Him. I'm biased because He's changed my life. You are at one of the finest universities in the United States, but if you don't learn about Jesus, you are not getting the best of educations. Will you look with me at a man who claimed to be God." And they looked. And week after week, I saw students fall in love with Him as we simply looked at the gospel of John together. In fact, hundreds of Christians now can trace their spiritual roots back to that little dorm Bible study. How did it happen? It was simple and yet so powerful – the gospel was the message. The same results can happen anywhere, and they will when our emphasis is not on ourselves or our own works, but when our message of first importance is Jesus Himself.

Questions for Discussion

1. Have you noticed a lack of evangelism in churches today? What has caused you to notice this?
2. Has there been a disillusionment in your own life when it comes to evangelism? What do you think has caused it?
3. What are some wrong motivations for evangelism that you have observed in others and yourself?
4. Have some of our methods of evangelism left you with more guilt than grace? Explain your answer.
5. Did you learn the five finger illustration? If so, what were the steps? Why do you think the steps changed among some people?
6. What has been the emphasis of most evangelistic approaches that you know?
7. Do you talk more about the church or Christ? Why do you think you have your emphasis?

Chapter Thirteen
swing vs. fire issues

"Swing versus Fire Issues," my counseling professor said. "It's the most important concept to understand in conflict resolutions."

All of us in the counseling class perked up when we heard that we were going to get one of those "most important" tidbits of helpful information. But at first I couldn't quite grasp the nature of how this lesson was so crucial to my counseling skills, much less my theology.

He explained that to understand how to solve problems you had to be able to discern how kids play in the backyard. When children are playing in the backyard, there are swing issues and fire issues. And a parent must always know the difference.

What are swing issues? A swing issue is when my little boy, Jeremy, goes out to the backyard and wants to play on the swing. He has never done it before, and I know what will happen if he does. Jeremy will start swinging with great anticipation. But after a few seconds, he will fall out of the swing, land on the gravel, and run to daddy, screaming. No, I couldn't let him experience such grief and pain. But I will. Because every little boy is going to swing one day, and there's got to be a first time. He will probably skin his knee. But skinned knees heal. He will cry, but the tears will dry. I will feel sorry for him for the moment, but it won't last very long. So there he is begging me to let him go on the swing. I can't fight him over it even though he may get hurt. Why? It's a swing issue.

The next day Jeremy wants to go into the backyard and play. Where? Not the swing this time, but where I'm burning trash. Am I going to let him? I let him play on the swing. He's got to learn about fire, doesn't he? So do I let him go play in the fire? No way! Fires don't skin knees. The damage of playing in a fire could be permanent. It might be irreparable. I put my foot down. He cannot play in the burning trash. Why? It's a fire issue.

What's the big deal about swing and fire issues? My professor told me that the problem with most people is that they can't distinguish between the swing and fire issues in their lives. In fact, most

SWING VS. FIRE ISSUES

people who have many conflicts have them because they treat every issue as a fire issue.

We are all going to have differing viewpoints and disagreements with other people. Some of them will be worth a fight. They are fire issues. Some of them won't be – they are swing issues. People who have lots of arguments usually treat every conflict as a fire issue. No matter what the disagreement is about, they fight over it. It doesn't take long for them to be like the boy who cried wolf. No one listens to their arguments anymore. Even if they have an important point, people don't listen because they have argued over everything in the past.

Understanding swing and fire issues is critical for good communication to take place in a marriage. I've seen some marriages fall apart when they never really had any overwhelming problems. The couple had simply learned to fight over everything. They treated every conflict like a fire issue. Squeezing versus rolling the toothpaste tube was fought over just as passionately as their purity. Conflicts will happen in marriages or any relationships. When they are all fought with equal intensity, the force of the arguments becomes overpowering.

To get along with people, one must be willing to give up or even lose on swing issues. They are just not as important. If someone fights about all the swing issues, no one can ever recognize what a fire issue is.

When I first got into ministry, everything was a

fire issue with me. I would fight with equal intensity over the order of worship as I would over the deity of Christ. Whether it was in an evangelistic encounter or a meeting with the elders, my objective was to win. The issue didn't matter. To lose a battle was seen as giving up my convictions. As a result, I fought needless battles and got a reputation of being hard to get along with. And the tragedy was that I lost some critical issues simply because I had won so many of the swing issues. Too often on the days of the fire issue, I was going to lose because people were ready for me to lose one.

It not only happens with individuals, it also happens with churches. I've seen church business meetings where the color of paint for the walls of the new educational wing was fought over with more passion than the spirituality of the teachers who would teach in it. I've been in meetings with church leaders where the mechanics of serving the Lord's Supper took precedence in time and concern over a person who had left the Lord. Again, we haven't distinguished between swing and fire issues in the church. Paint and the mechanics of order in an assembly are swing issues. The content of our teaching and a person's relationship to God are fire issues. Jesus taught that some things are great and others are weightier. In other words, there are some fire issues, and we need to know what they are.

The tendency of most of us who have a problem here is to make fire issues out of swing issues.

Most divisions and church splits occur when a swing issue is treated with the fervor that ought to be reserved for fire issues. But the other side of the coin is still possible. We could act like there are not any fire issues. Making every issue a fire issue usually comes from a lack of understanding God's grace. It is when every issue is of equal importance and to lose any of them would be equally threatening that we miss God's grace. If salvation is based upon our own righteousness and correctness, then every issue would be worth fighting over. We couldn't afford to lose even one. But if our salvation is based upon the righteousness of God and His grace, then there must be a value system based upon God's importance and a graciousness demonstrated to others as He has given to us.

However, some who have rejected legalism and a righteousness rooted in our own merit have swung too far. Everything is not a swing issue. There are some fire issues. A rejection of legalism does not insure a discovery of grace. In a rejection of legalism, one will often adopt a laissez faire commitment to freedom. It is a freedom based upon the attitude of acceptance at all costs. When everything becomes a swing issue and there are no longer fire issues, we have not found grace.

On the front page of a student newspaper at the University of Washington, a question was posed – "Is There Anything Worth Dying For?" The paper interviewed students on their opinion of the giving of human life. A remarkable number of campus people concluded that there was nothing worth dying for. In other words, there were no fire issues. Although most of their responses related to war, it was interesting to note how a segment of society had opted for pacifism at all costs. Isn't there anything left worth dying for? Isn't there anything left worth fighting for? Jesus thought so. Grace demands it. It was grace that brought the Son of God to die on the cross. Was it in vain? Certainly those of us bought by the blood of Christ would say people saved by that sacrifice are worth fighting and even dying for.

It's always bothered me that in some songbooks they've changed the words to "The Battle Hymn of the Republic." In the line that says, "As He died to make men holy, let us die to make men free," the word "die" was changed to "teach." It's true that our teaching can bring freedom. But isn't there anything worth dying for anymore? A rank spiritual pacificism that produces freedom without commitment and conviction can hardly be grace. Grace brings freedom, but it doesn't end commitment. Grace breaks down the walls of human authoritarianism, but it doesn't end spiritual leadership. It's possible to become legalistic about freedom. One could judge anyone's hard work, commitment, and structure as signs of spiritual repression. But if their motivation is out of love rather than an enforcement by a leader or a meritorious act, then it is good, gracious, and hardly an opponent of freedom. Even freedom fighters need to allow others the freedom to disagree.

That's grace.

We have fought too much. And we have fought over the wrong things. We have hidden a feuding spirit under the hat of "contending for the faith." But even when Jude speaks of contending for the faith, is he merely talking about a body of issues or is faith also the trust we have in the Father and the way we are to walk in our lives? When I studied Jude in school, we referred to it as "The Acts of the Apostates." I remember that the chief quest of our study was to find out who the apostates were. If the examples given in Jude bear out the secret of apostasy and reveal who isn't contending for the faith, it becomes evident that the apostates aren't unbelievers outside the church. No, they are those inside the church who are not corrupted as much by their stance on the issues as they are in their attitude on them. They are the ones, like the Israelites on the exodus who become divisive because of their grumbling and complaining. Probably no verse describes this problem better than Jude 16: "These are grumblers, finding fault, following after their own lusts; they speak arrogantly, flattering people for the sake of gaining an advantage."

The real apostates are the ones that are constantly finding fault. They have a grumbling spirit. You have met them before, haven't you? They always have to find out every little thing that is wrong and point it out. They think that their spiritual gift is to debug the church like a computer programmer does when the program is written. He has to go over it again and again to get all the bugs out or to correct any errors. But God never mentions debugging as a ministry of the church. He's against a critical, fault-finding spirit.

Jude's apostate "flatters people for the sake of gaining advantage." I call these people "spiritual Eddie Haskells." You remember him from "Leave it to Beaver," don't you? He was always flattering Mrs. Cleaver so he could get what he wanted. I'm talking about church politics here. It's where people buddy up to church leaders and play politics to get things their way whether it's a fire issue or not. It's going behind people's backs and being deceptive to get your way on your issue. That's not contending for the faith. It's the very apostasy that's condemned.

When a critical, fault-finding spirit plays church politics with swing issues, we are far from the focus. Once again, it's a proper understanding of God's grace that keeps us from developing this attitude and mentality. I think our only hope for stopping the division and starting the healing in the church is to go back and have a good look at God's grace.

By grace we have been saved. By grace we must live. Some things are more important than others in our lives. Grace is one of them. It's not a swing issue. It's in the heart of the fire.

SWING VS. FIRE ISSUES

Questions for Discussion.

1. Name some swing issues.
2. What issues would you call fire issues?
3. What are some swing issues that you have fought about as if they were fire issues?
4. What are some fire issues that you have treated as if they were swing issues?
5. In what areas have we allowed freedom to evolve into complacency?
6. Where have you seen a critical, fault-finding spirit in the church? What can you do about it?
7. How do we play church politics? Why should grace keep us from doing this?